OBJECT LESSONS AND EARLY LEARNING

The twenty-first century is a time of change for early learning in museums, due in part to society's evolving view of childhood, from an age of innocence to understanding the robust learning that defines the first years of life. This perspective is a catalyst for international conversation and continues to raise attention and interest across society. *Object Lessons and Early Learning* leverages what is known about the cognitive development of young children to examine the power of learning through objects in museum and heritage settings.

Exploring the history and modern day practice of object-based learning, Shaffer outlines the rationale for endorsing this approach in both formal and informal learning spaces. She argues that museums, as collecting institutions, are learning spaces uniquely positioned to allow children to make meaning about their world through personal connections to cultural artifacts, natural specimens, and works of art. A range of descriptive object lessons, inspired by objects in museums as well as from the everyday world, are presented throughout the text as examples of ways in which children can be encouraged to engage with museum collections.

Object Lessons and Early Learning offers insights into strategies for engaging young children as learners in museum settings and in their everyday world, and, as such, will be essential reading for museum professionals, classroom educators, and students. It should also be of great interest to academics and researchers engaged in the study of museums and education.

Sharon E. Shaffer is a museum consultant specializing in providing programming to younger children and works with museum professionals around the world. She is a former Executive Director of the Smithsonian Early Enrichment Center, USA, and is the only educator ever to receive the Smithsonian Institution Secretary's Gold Medal for Exceptional Service. She has a PhD in Social Foundations of Education and is an adjunct faculty member with the University of Virginia.

OBJECT LESSONS AND EARLY LEARNING

Sharon E. Shaffer

NEW YORK AND LONDON

First published 2018
by Routledge
711 Third Avenue, New York, NY 10017

and by Routledge
2 Park Square, Milton Park, Abingdon, Oxon OX14 4RN

Routledge is an imprint of the Taylor & Francis Group, an informa business

© 2018 Taylor & Francis

The right of Sharon E. Shaffer to be identified as author of this work has been asserted by her in accordance with sections 77 and 78 of the Copyright, Designs and Patents Act 1988.

All rights reserved. No part of this book may be reprinted or reproduced or utilised in any form or by any electronic, mechanical, or other means, now known or hereafter invented, including photocopying and recording, or in any information storage or retrieval system, without permission in writing from the publishers.

Trademark notice: Product or corporate names may be trademarks or registered trademarks, and are used only for identification and explanation without intent to infringe.

Library of Congress Cataloging-in-Publication Data
A catalog record for this title has been requested

ISBN: 978-1-62958-404-1 (hbk)
ISBN: 978-1-62958-405-8 (pbk)
ISBN: 978-0-203-70225-3 (ebk)

Typeset in Bembo
by Taylor & Francis Books

CONTENTS

List of illustrations   *vii*
Acknowledgments   *viii*
Preface   *x*

SECTION I
Object Lessons in Theory: A Key to Interpretation

1 Setting the Stage for Early Learning in Museums   1

2 The Museum Object: A Story of Change   15

3 The Object Lesson: A Closer Look at Its History and Development   31

4 Object-Based Learning: Making Meaning from Objects   45

SECTION II
Theory to Practice: Young Children and Objects

5 Learning to Look at Objects: A Process of Discovery   57

6 Curiosity and Collections: A Child's Perspective   73

SECTION III
Object Lessons: Engaging Young Museum Visitors

7 Object Lessons Inspired by History Museums and Historic Homes   83

8 Object Lessons Inspired by Art Museums, Sculpture Gardens, and Public Art   97

9 Object Lessons Inspired by Cultural Exhibitions and Institutions   113

SECTION IV
Object Lessons Beyond the Gallery

10 Object Lessons for Young Learners in School Settings   127

SECTION V
A Look Forward

11 The Future of Early Learning in a Digital Society: Finding a Balance between Object-Based Experiences and Technology   138

References   *150*
Index   *157*

ILLUSTRATIONS

Figures

1.1	Hein's model for educational theories	8
1.2	The Early Learning Model (ELM)	9
1.3	Young child engaged in art making	10
2.1	The Children's Museum of Indianapolis. Family looking at the Max Simon comic book collection in the Galleries for American Arts and Popular Culture	29
3.1	Froebel's first gift: hand-crocheted balls	37
4.1	Primitive soap saver	49
4.2	Mojaris, Hyderabad, c. 1790–1820	54
5.1	Nature: Stackable Leaves	68
5.2	Nature: I See a Nest	68
5.3	Nature: A Bug Lives Here	69
6.1	Young toddler curious about a collection of postcards	76
7.1	Knife box with lock from Montpelier Collection	88
8.1	Children enjoy the interactive installation "Los Trompos" ("The Spinning Tops") on the High Museum of Art's Carroll Slater Sifly Piazza. Created by Mexican designers Héctor Esrawe and Ignacio Cadena, the site-specific installation was commissioned by the High as part of its multi-year initiative to activate the Museum's outdoor space.	100

ACKNOWLEDGMENTS

The journey of writing a book is not one traveled alone, but a collaborative effort that includes contributions from many, some actively engaged in this process and others unknowingly inspiring the words and the content. None are insignificant and all are cherished.

I am in awe of the many museum educators who have taken up the mantle of early learning and embraced young children as important visitors to museums. Their work comes from the heart and is a gift to the children and families they touch.

In my work as a consultant I have been blessed by the opportunities to know and learn from colleagues engaged in projects that impact the lives of young children, many in America but others from around the world. It has been a privilege to work collaboratively with Dr. Ni Zhang, Executive Director for the Children's Museum Research Center (CMRC) in Beijing, a leader making a difference in the lives of children in China by introducing children's museums to the nation. Sharing ideas and a passion for early learning with Ni reminds me of the value of this work. I am thankful for talented colleagues around the world dedicated to young children and opportunities to experience the world through museums.

Important to the writing process is the feedback garnered from trusted colleagues in the field, each taking personal time to read and respond to some aspect of the book. Their insights and suggestions are invaluable and add significantly to the final text. Readers that I want to thank are Nicole Cromartie, Elee Wood, Marjorie Schwartzer, Cynthia Raso, Alyson Williams, Isabelle Alessandra, Allison Wickens, Anna Hindley, Donna Tobey, and Julia Forbes. I also appreciate the work of colleagues who authored short complementary narratives related to a specific topic as well as those who worked behind the scenes for permissions for images. A special thanks to Kristen Buckley and Heather Fanberg for their contributions.

I want to thank the many museum professionals adding their voices to *Object Lessons and Early Learning* through participation in questionnaires, AAM's Open

Forum, and individual interviews, with particular thanks to Laura Huerta Migus, Beth Fitzgerald, Susan Foutz, Petrushka Bazin Larsen, Loretta Yajima, Sunnee O'Rork, Elee Wood, Jenny Sweeney, Tiffany Allen, Barbara Meyerson, Rebecca Hertz, Barbara Franco, Lee Gambol, Christina Bulow, Kristi Lucas-Hayden, Ted Lind, Dale Hilton, Betsy Bowers, and Ni Zhang. Their words and insightful thoughts introduce a perspective to the discussion of early learning that is important in the twenty-first century. The list of every valued colleague is far too long to include here, but their work continues to be a gift that influences my thinking. I want to thank each and every one for making a difference for young children in museums.

This endeavor of writing would not be possible without the love and support of my family. I am forever grateful to my husband, Mark, for his day-to-day support and encouragement. My children and their partners, and certainly, my wonderful grandchildren inspire me to share my passion about early learning in museums as a means of making a difference in the world. It is with great appreciation that I dedicate this book to the ones I love.

PREFACE

> Fill your paper with the breathings of your heart.
>
> *William Wordsworth*

Object Lessons and Early Learning represents a labor of love, a reflection of the passion that I have for young children and the unimaginable opportunities for learning in museums. As Wordsworth suggests, the ideas written on the pages of this book are truly breathings of my heart.

I am one of the fortunate ones, someone who followed her dreams, and in doing so, discovered a unique path in education that was more exciting than I could ever have imagined. In 1988, I joined the Smithsonian Institution and stepped into the role of founding director for the Smithsonian's lab school for young children, the Smithsonian Early Enrichment Center, and discovered a new and exciting world of learning that offered children opportunities to explore art, history, science, and culture through artifacts and natural specimens displayed in museum galleries. Not only were the environments and their exhibitions rich in treasures, but the experts at the Institution added another dimension to the experience with a few inviting our children behind the scenes for an insider's view. It became apparent over time that these were defining moments for many of our preschoolers, setting the stage for the future.

In the 1980s and 1990s, young children were infrequent visitors in traditional museums and seldom were viewed by museum professionals as part of the mainstream audience. Since that time, groundbreaking discoveries by neuroscientists and researchers brought attention to cognitive development in the early years, stimulating interest in exploring the potential for children's learning in museums. In many ways, this was the catalyst for changing society's view of early learning, a pivotal moment in time that opened the door to new conversations leading to change in museums.

The story of preschoolers and kindergartners in the twenty-first century is no longer one of marginalization, but rather a story of triumph where children are honored and respected as learners. More and more, museum professionals are part of that chorus of support and are experimenting with new ideas and techniques to engage this growing audience. But success for this new wave of thinking is not defined simply by a desire to serve young audiences, but rather is bound by a true desire to understand the learning style of children which means acquiring knowledge of educational theory as a necessary foundation on which to build effective and appropriate practice. Knowledge of theory guides practitioners to go beyond intuitive practice and opens minds to more insightful programming that takes into account developmental characteristics of the audience, in this case, young children. Theories of learning cannot be overlooked as inconsequential to practitioners, but viewed instead as a cornerstone for the design and implementation of experiences for young learners.

Object Lessons and Early Learning builds on the ideas of *Engaging Young Children in Museums*, but narrows the scope and focus on the concept of learning through objects. Object-based learning, also referred to in the context of object lessons, is not new, but spans centuries. It is an idea of lasting integrity, essential to museums and their dedication to objects.

Object Lessons and Early Learning offers educators and museum professionals a framework for thinking about teaching with objects in today's world with specific examples of lessons inspired by artifacts or works of art in museums as well as in the everyday world of the young child. Lessons concentrate on art, history, and culture and are a reflection of collections that challenge the educator new to working with young audiences. The lessons presented in the text are intended to be broad-based experiences with strategies applicable to science and nature centers as well as children's museums and other collecting institutions. Although object lessons are described in detail, the description is intended as a narrative of possibilities rather than a prescriptive approach for educators. These lessons begin with a framework for understanding a child's approach to constructing knowledge and include a range of opportunities for exploring ideas through objects. The learning experience is best understood as a fluid process where the interests and interpretations of children are valued and allowed to shape the museum experience. The object lessons serve as a model with possibilities for the journey of exploration, but approached with the understanding that the actual experience will flow from the ideas of the children and will likely deviate from the prepared lesson. Flexibility is key; the program is most effective when it reflects the responses of the children. Listening to children and their ideas is the basis for early learning programming in museums or schools.

It's an exciting time for early learning as more and more museums around the globe extend their welcome to young children, even greeting toddlers and babies with enthusiasm as they enter galleries. The nature of children's learning is integrally connected to interaction with the things of the world where exploration through the senses leads to personal meaning-making and construction of knowledge.

Object lessons still have relevance for today's thinking about learning. At a time of technological advancement and immersive experiences in virtual reality, it is important to consider the role of objects in learning, particularly for the young child. Are objects still critical to a young child's learning? What does this mean for children as learners in museums in this age of high technology? Through the voices of museum professionals and more broadly educators in a range of environments, *Object Lessons and Early Learning* begins a conversation about technology and children's learning, at least on a cursory level, recognizing that this is a topic that deserves greater attention in the future.

My hope is to encourage educators and museum professionals to explore possibilities for engaging young children with objects and to look at their institution's collections with a new perspective, keeping young children in mind. There are exceptional models and programs that can serve as inspiration for those interested in early learning.

As professionals, let's reach out to colleagues across the museum community to share ideas and learn from one another and serve as ambassadors for younger audiences. Not only can we share experiences, but we can learn from practitioners in the field by collecting and sharing data for analysis. With support from formal research partners, we can grow in our understanding and be better able to create a meaningful place for early learning in museums. By working together we'll be shaping new beginnings for children and their lifetime relationship with museums.

1

SETTING THE STAGE FOR EARLY LEARNING IN MUSEUMS

> All of us have moments in our childhood where we come alive for the first time. And we go back to those moments and think, "This is when I became myself."
>
> *Rita Dove*

Introduction

Museums are magical places for most people. For the young child, an environment filled with familiar and unfamiliar objects becomes a place of wonder and excitement, transporting the child to new worlds through the power of imagination. Museums with their awe-inspiring experiences are places that offer life-changing moments for young visitors. As Rita Dove suggests in the above quote, we all have defining moments in childhood that come to define who we are later in life. An early encounter in a museum might be that magical moment when a child is inspired to be a botanist, archaeologist, or artist. It is the beginning of something new and wonderful!

In many ways, museums are made for children. A young child's ability to suspend reality and imagine another place or time is useful in making connections to art and artifacts. Although children understand their world in a way that is qualitatively different from adults, they are able to interpret what they see by making associations with prior knowledge. Children's intuitive strategies become tools that build a foundation for learning about their world and how it works.

Children in the twenty-first century are welcomed into many museums and inspired by art and artifacts, but this has not always been so. Museums are clearly in a time of change (Schwarzer 2006) from how they tell stories through objects to ways they connect with the public and the diversity of people they serve.

The museum is no longer defined by its walls and galleries, but extends into the community to touch the lives of people, both young and old, in many diverse ways. It is no longer solely about the object, but more importantly now is focused on the story. A child in the twenty-first century will understand museums in a way that differs from that of past generations, reflecting a realm of interactions that range from art and artifacts in galleries and sculpture gardens to digital interfaces with objects and experiences that take place outside of the walls of museums. This change certainly influences how we perceive the young child in the context of museums.

At a time when museum attendance is declining (National Endowment for the Arts 2013) or at best leveling off (Falk and Dierking 2013), anecdotal accounts by museum professionals show a significant increase in the public's desire for children's programs and experiences, particularly those aimed at preschoolers and babies. This is true both in the United States and abroad. Young museum-goers are visiting traditional museums with families and preschool classes more frequently now than ever before. They are experiencing art, artifacts, and natural specimens through educational programs, specially designed spaces that engage learners through their senses, and hands-on opportunities offered in galleries and during family festivals.

Each experience becomes more meaningful when it is relevant for a child. But how is relevance defined for the young museum visitor? The idea of *relevance* is frequently referenced in today's conversations, part of the lexicon of most individuals. But at times it's a word that is bandied about without much thought to its meaning. When thinking about young children in museums, relevance can be defined as a place of intersection between the child's world and the collection. It is that sweet spot for making meaning where a child's background knowledge derived from past experience and the specific collection represented in a museum come together. This place of intersection grows, and knowledge deepens, with new encounters; meaning comes from making connections between the known and the unknown to build new understanding.

Relevance can be as simple as a preschooler's experience with Calder's sculpture of a fish, a work of art crafted from wire and found objects. The sculpture, while novel, retains familiar features such as shape or texture, so that a child can easily associate this new object with the real thing based on previous encounters with books or personal experiences. For some children, there is a clear connection between the scales of a real fish and the wire framework of the sculpture housing each found object from a piece of sea glass or a gear to a broken shell, all connections to prior knowledge that allow a child to construct meaning. And while a child's understanding of the art is far from comprehensive in nature, meaningful connections are made as children integrate each new experience with knowledge from the past. The interpretive process is in play, even at a very early age.

There are often misconceptions about a child's ability to relate to unfamiliar objects, which leads to excluding children from exhibitions or even museums that represent collections outside of a child's existing experience. This is particularly true for children five years of age or younger. But relevance is still possible, even with unfamiliar objects. The secret is finding that place of intersection with a child's world.

With unknown artifacts, educators and parents can facilitate learning by introducing familiar objects to enlighten the child about the less familiar entity. An artifact such as an African headrest, clearly an unfamiliar object for most children, can be understood when associated with a small pillow, a familiar object. There is often a moment of excitement when a young child recognizes the relationship between the familiar and unfamiliar objects. Experiences gain relevance when connections are made between a child's world and the new encounter.

Today's museum educators likely recognize the value of creating children's experiences that connect with a child's interests or prior knowledge, thereby increasing the likelihood that the experience is relevant for young visitors. But has this practice always been a part of museum education? What does the history of museums tell us about the place of children in these institutions?

A Look Back: Children in Museums

The American museum of the eighteenth century is not the museum of today. From the 1773 collection gathered by the Charleston Library Society to the first public museum in 1786 in the Philadelphia home of artist Charles Wilson Peale (Schwarzer 2006, p. 8), the era of museums took root. Today's museum is strikingly different from that of early museums, from the demographics of visitors to the physical design of the space as well as expectations of what the experience might be. Unlike the static displays in early libraries and museums, current exhibitions seek to engage the visitor in the story and in some cases invite community collaboration in the creation of stories and exhibitions. In the past two centuries, the museum as an institution has grown and transformed as a reflection of the values and beliefs of society.

The early history of the American museum can be defined in terms of collections displayed in the homes of the wealthy, comprised of artifacts gathered from travel or objects that reflect a collector's personal curiosity, often specimens from nature. Artifacts were loosely organized and shared primarily with friends of a similar social class; displays were often described as cabinets of curiosities and reserved for members of the social elite. Over time, collections moved from private parlors to libraries, becoming some of the first public exhibitions (ibid.), and then to venues designed specifically for collection display.

Children entered the scene when museums formalized their commitment to education in institutional mission statements and invested in exhibitions and programs designed to serve the public. "Through the display of objects, museum directors desired to make meaningful learning experiences accessible to the masses. Exhibitions were viewed as vehicles to advance the arts and sciences and to edify aesthetic taste and public moral values" (Findlay and Perricone 2009, p. 8). And while reaching the masses was the aim, many minorities and groups from lower socio-economic levels of society were not included. Even so, the demographics defining the museum audience were changing, beginning to represent a broader swath of society that included school children. Museums welcomed a more diverse audience into their halls and galleries to learn from the collections. Over time, society came to view these institutions as places of learning.

At a time when traditional museums were still perceived primarily as places for scholarly research or leisure activity for the well-educated, the Smithsonian Institution offered a somewhat different view for the museum field, one that advanced the Institution's commitment to education. Under the visionary leadership of Samuel P. Langley (1887–1906), the Smithsonian Institution created The Children's Room, devoting time and resources to reach a more diverse audience, specifically children. Langley's efforts began in 1889 with "experiments in the ornithological department," intended to create more child-friendly experiences (NeCastro 1988, p. 2). Although Secretary Langley was disappointed with this early experiment, he understood that "if children were to benefit from the educational possibilities which existed in museums, a different approach to exhibit design would be necessary" (ibid., p. 2). This insight informed the design and planning for The Children's Room, which opened in 1901 in the south tower of the Smithsonian's Castle. The space was designed especially for children and their unique style of learning, filled with objects that might appeal to a child's interests, a rectangular aquarium with live fish, songbirds in golden cages, eggs, feathers, minerals, and fossils, all at a child's height (Shaffer 2015). Scientific labels written in Latin were discarded in favor of simple, familiar text. Careful thought was given to every aspect of the space, from the color of walls and floor tiles to the amount of light entering through windows (NeCastro 1988). Langley's interests went far beyond the idea of an exhibition as an opportunity for learning. His purpose was to create a space "to excite the wonder and curiosity of children, to inspire them unconsciously with a love of nature" (Smithsonian Institution 1902, p. 54).

Langley was not the only museum professional thinking about the potential impact of museums on children's learning. William H. Goodyear, a curator from the Brooklyn Institute of Arts and Sciences in New York, was leading an effort to create a museum designed specifically for children. This newly formed entity, known as the Brooklyn Children's Museum, marked a milestone in the history of museums and defined a groundbreaking movement that would grow to international success over the next century. With a small collection of less than perfect artifacts donated by the Brooklyn Institute of Arts and Sciences, the first children's museum opened to the community in 1899 and created a more child-friendly environment for learning from objects. The popularity of the Brooklyn Children's Museum, and later the Boston Children's Museum (1913), set the tone for other communities interested in designing museums that catered to the interests and learning style of the young.

Early children's museums were collecting institutions created to serve a young audience, but differed from the more traditional museum in that they adopted a hands-on approach to learning where visitors were free to experience the sensory nature of objects. Visitors could "sort, polish, and examine" (Hein 2006, p. 166) rocks and minerals in open collections and make personal discoveries through exploration of artifacts and specimens. The children's museum emphasized observation and reflection as a means of developing an understanding of the world.

By the turn of the twentieth century, new partnerships between museums and schools were developing to give school-aged children an opportunity to learn from museum collections. Field trips, or journeys, became popular for teachers wanting to enrich the student experience through the use of real objects representing specific areas of study (Findlay and Perricone 2009). This popularity continued throughout much of the twentieth century. Partnerships also led to school museums, which garnered support from educators as a means of enhancing curriculum. In this time of social progressivism, museums were paying attention to the education of school children. And although traditional museums welcomed older children into their galleries as a result of these partnerships, preschool children rarely visited these institutions, relegated almost exclusively to children's museums.

By mid-century the nation's museums were responding to social issues and world events such as Russia's 1957 launch of Sputnik. The American public as well as government officials looked toward education as a solution to political failings and social ills (Tyack and Cuban 1995), and museums as educational institutions took note. The country placed an emphasis on science and mathematics to regain its role as a world leader which ultimately led to a plethora of science-related museums and a new way of thinking about learning in these public venues. At the Exploratorium in San Francisco, Frank Oppenheimer designed exhibitions that encouraged exploration and discovery by visitors, changing the previous dynamic within galleries (Oppenheimer 1968). His innovative methods emphasizing sensory perception as a means of learning spread widely, introducing museums to the idea of a more active role for visitors. Oppenheimer's techniques, while intended for all audiences, held great appeal for families and younger audiences with the emphasis on sensory experience.

Others in the field added to the idea of active learning in museums. Michael Spock, Director of the Boston Children's Museum, embraced the notion of "experiential learning and the joys of touching" (Madden and Paisley-Jones 1987, p. 2), an approach that, while foreign to most traditional museums, was now under consideration. Discovery rooms in natural history museums, discovery carts with touchable objects, and specially-designed spaces that allowed for exploration grew from Spock's ideas and became the norm in many museums. With the inclusion of hands-on experiences, museums were viewed as more family-friendly places with opportunities to engage younger children.

In the 1960s, beliefs about young children and their potential to learn shifted with the country's emphasis on early childhood education and the launch of Head Start programs stemming from President Lyndon Johnson's War on Poverty. Research on the effects of poverty on children and the impact of education contributed to more informed views of children and the need for education at an early age. By the 1990s, technological advances allowed researchers to study the brain (Shore 1997) to understand learning in the early years. Breakthroughs in neuroscience added to knowledge from previous research on early childhood education which redefined views about the significance of learning in the first years of life. Early learning was on the rise with new beliefs about the value of early experience garnered through research and study.

The 1992 publication of *Excellence and Equity: Education and the Public Dimension of Museums* (American Association of Museums 1992) added to the conversation about children in museums by redefining education in the field. The AAM report stressed the need for museums to serve a more diverse audience, which ultimately led to expanded programming for all ages, abilities, and ethnicities. Young children marched into museums on the coattails of *Excellence and Equity*.

Interest in young children and the early years of learning grew as the twentieth century ended. The Association of Children's Museums filled a niche within American society by contributing to the education of children in informal environments, advancing the idea of play as a mode of learning. Model programs in museums, such as the Smithsonian Early Enrichment Center (SEEC) and the Philadelphia Museum of Art's *Museum Looks and Picture Books*, offered further evidence that young children have the capacity to learn from art and artifacts in gallery settings. Support for early learning grew in ways unfathomable only a few decades before, representing a wide range of individuals and organizations from politicians and national media to local school boards and parents. Early learning's star was on the rise.

Museums have not always been a place for very young children. But many of today's museums are welcoming preschoolers and babies into their galleries and hoping to create experiences that are meaningful for these young museum visitors. The aim is to create relevant experiences that truly engage the young learner. To accomplish that goal, it is critical to understand educational theory and to design practice based on that understanding.

Educational Theory and Practice

Learning holds a place of importance in museums and plays a prominent role throughout much of the field's history. This is evidenced by mission statements across time, each promising a commitment to education and learning through their collections, and also voiced by leaders representing larger museums as well as smaller, less-known institutions. The message of education rings true in the mission statement of the Smithsonian Institution's National Museum of Natural History: "We increase knowledge and inspire learning about nature and culture, through outstanding research, collections, exhibitions, and education, in support of a sustainable future" (Smithsonian Institution 2015). It is equally present in the Kluge-Ruhe Aboriginal Art Collection of the University of Virginia, a small museum committed to learning: "Our mission is to advance knowledge and understanding of Australia's Indigenous people and their art and culture worldwide" (Kluge-Ruhe Aboriginal Art Collection of the University of Virginia 2015). Learning and museums are intertwined.

Since education is central to museums, it is important to consider the role of educational theory in the work of museum professionals. It is not sufficient for educators to work from a point of intuition, even though this approach may at times be fruitful. Rather, theory provides insight that can be applied not only in the planning process, but also in implementation. When educational spaces seem less than inviting to young children or program strategies fail to engage little ones, theory brings perspective that educators can use to resolve problems.

Hein's Model of Educational Theory

George E. Hein, a preeminent voice in cognitive theory and author of numerous books and articles, including *Learning in the Museum* (Hein 1998), writes about educational theories and suggests that each institution adopt a conceptual framework of learning to provide continuity and guide practice for its organization. An educational framework provides guidance in answering important questions that relate to the work of the institution. How do people learn? Which factors are likely to motivate or engage learners? What are the responsibilities of museums in shaping learning? These questions and others can be considered in the context of educational theory.

Learning theories are not a new phenomenon, but are reflected in the ideas and practices of people from the times of ancient Greece to modern theorists. Theories that describe how people process, integrate, and construct meaning about the world are complex and dynamic, often reflecting social and cultural beliefs as well as the values of a particular time or place. Beliefs about learning that are strongly held in one decade may lose credibility over time as new ideas are introduced or they may be widely accepted, then diminish in importance only to become popular again at a later date.

In *Learning in the Museum* (ibid.), Hein describes in detail a model that shows the intersection of two components of educational theory: the nature of knowledge (epistemology) and the psychology of learning. This intersection defines four "possible combinations of learning theory and epistemology" (Hein 1995, p. 22) with each quadrant representing a specific approach to learning (Figure 1.1).

Beliefs about knowledge are expressed along a continuum and vary from realism to idealism (extremes of the continuum). Realism is viewed as an absolute where knowledge exists in the external world, apart from the learner. Idealism suggests that knowledge is constructed within the individual, uniquely formed by a variety of factors. Similarly, concepts related to learning represent end points from passive, incremental learning to actively constructing knowledge. The former position "assumes that learning consists of the incremental assimilation of information, facts, and experiences, until knowledge results" (ibid., p. 21). The latter view recognizes that concepts develop within the mind and are the product of myriad sensorial experiences which include social, cultural, and environmental encounters.

Hein's model serves as a framework for understanding different perspectives on educational theory, driven by beliefs about the nature of knowledge and the psychology of learning. The quadrants represent different approaches to learning: didactic, expository approach; discovery learning; stimulus-response; and

8 Setting the Stage: Early Learning in Museums

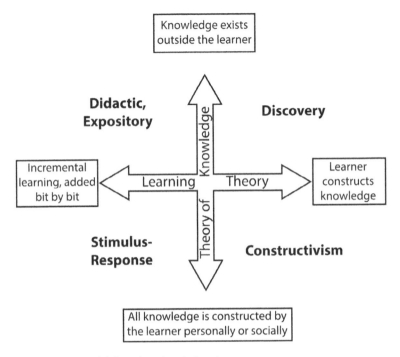

FIGURE 1.1 Hein's model for educational theories
Source: Redrawn from Hein (1998).

constructivism. While volumes have been written about educational theory, Hein's model is valuable in that it encourages educators and other museum practitioners to reflect on their own beliefs about learning and recognize the importance of aligning practice with beliefs.

Constructivist Theory and Young Children

Constructivist theory is the learning framework that receives most attention from twenty-first-century educators in the United States and other western cultures. It is heralded as the most effective means for engaging visitors of all ages in museums, but is equally praised for classroom learning. The ideas are particularly apt when thinking about the active learning style of younger children.

The Early Learning Model (ELM) is situated within a constructivist approach to learning and describes the behaviors of a child engaged in the process of learning (Figure 1.2). Knowledge is constructed through a dynamic process when children explore, experience, conceptualize, imagine, and create. The process, while not linear, often begins with a child's innate curiosity which leads to exploration and in turn experiencing the world through her senses. As information is internalized and synthesis occurs, concepts or schema are created. A child builds on internalized concepts and imagines the role, place, or interdependencies of

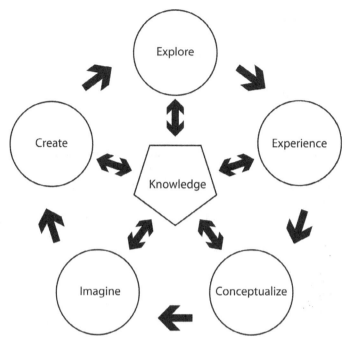

FIGURE 1.2 The Early Learning Model (ELM)

concepts while often creating new understandings or ideas. ELM offers a practical model for understanding how a child constructs knowledge about her world.

Constructivist learning theory grounds educators in museums and in schools when designing programs or lessons. What is the role of the child in the experience? What are the anticipated behaviors that support that claim? Are there elements in the program that are child-centered, allowing for choice based on interests? Are children's ideas and opinions valued? Is the museum activity connected in some way to children's prior knowledge or past experience? Is there flexibility in the program? How is success defined?

Museums strive to create environments that inspire, teach, and engage the public through collections and educational programs. Constructivist learning theory is valued as a method that supports those ideals.

Themes of Learning Theory

Constructivism is not a new idea, but rather reimagined in today's social and historical context. It is the contemporary view of learning that suggests "people construct new knowledge and understanding based on what they already know and believe" (National Research Council 2000). John Dewey, Jean Piaget, Lev Vygotsky, Maria Montessori, Jerome Bruner, and Howard Gardner are but a few of the individuals whose beliefs influence educators through explanations of how knowledge is constructed. Their ideas, and those of others in the field, can be ascribed to the individual or can be synthesized across theorists and organized by theme, in the case of this overview, four themes: (1) the nature of experience; (2) play; (3) ways of knowing; and (4) motivation and learning.

Theme I: The Nature of Experience

Experience is probably the most prominent characteristic associated with constructivist learning and often thought of as sensory in nature. From the earliest moments of life, children explore the world through their senses – sight, sound, taste, touch, and smell – and internalize information from those interactions to ultimately construct meaning about their world (Figure 1.3).

This concept of experience is probably most noteworthy in the work of prominent American philosopher, John Dewey (1859–1952), whose writings reveal experience to be the primary path for learning. And while this is so, Dewey suggests that every experience is not educative and that interaction with the environment is not sufficient for learning. For Dewey, it is reflection on and application of knowledge to future endeavors that make an experience educative (Dewey 1916). "Education must be conceived as a continuing reconstruction of experience" (Dewey 1897). The idea that learning requires cognitive engagement as well as sensorial experience is also a guiding principle espoused by Dewey that resonates with educators today.

As the ideas of Dewey gained prominence in America, Russian psychologist, Lev Vygotsky (1896–1934) developed his own theories of learning and advanced the idea of a meaningful link between language and experience, noting "The

FIGURE 1.3 Young child engaged in art making

sensory material and the word are both indispensable parts of concept formation" (Vygotsky [1962] 1986, pp. 96–97). For Vygotsky, experience is the teacher. He further suggests that culture influences how an individual perceives and constructs meaning.

In Vygotsky's writings, experience is broadly construed and includes social interaction as perhaps the most important aspect contributing to the construction of knowledge to the point of suggesting that all learning is socially mediated. To explain the role of social interaction in learning, Vygotsky introduced a concept described as *the zone of proximal development (ZPD)*. This concept defines baseline performance where an individual works independently and an upper limit where success is unattainable even with guidance or support. These two boundaries establish the optimal learning zone (ZPD) where a child experiences challenges beyond his independent capabilities and successfully manages the experience with *scaffolding* or support from a more knowledgeable peer or adult. Educators with an understanding of this concept are able to design a lesson or museum experience that challenges a child to achieve at a higher level of learning, while staying within boundaries to avoid frustration. This idea is recognized for its merits by educators in museums and schools, and certainly holds true for young learners.

Any discussion of experience requires a look at the work of Swiss psychologist, Jean Piaget (1896–1980), a theorist who recognized the impact of the senses on learning, particularly noting their significance in the early years. Piaget's belief in a child's agency in learning is evident when he states, "each time one prematurely teaches a child something he could have discovered for himself, that child is kept from inventing it and, consequently, from understanding it completely" (Piaget 1970, p. 715). In his writing, Piaget advances the idea of *assimilation* and *accommodation* as a process for concept development. *Assimilation* is the process of taking in information through interactions with the environment to build mental images or constructs, termed *schema* by Piaget. Comparisons are made to what is known from previous experiences and ideas with the intent to fit into an already existing schema. *Accommodation* is a complementary process whereby mental constructs are refined based on new encounters if the information conflicts with concepts already present. Mental constructs continue to evolve as new experiences are compared to existing concepts and refined to reach a balance or equilibrium based on all experience. Assimilation and accommodation are complementary processes within adaptation.

Learning through sensory experience is also highlighted in the work of Maria Montessori (1870–1952), the first female physician in Italy and creator of Casa del Bambini, a school dedicated to teaching preschool children. Montessori created sensory-rich, child-centered materials for solving problems and mastering concepts. In Montessori schools, children learn letters by tracing tactile models, stack blocks sequentially to build a pink tower, and compare textures to identify matching materials. Experience and the senses are viewed as integrally intertwined.

An overview of experience would not be complete without mentioning Jerome Bruner (1915–2016), a theorist who advanced the idea of experience as transformational for the individual and underscored discovery as an essential experiential tool for learning to solve problems and answer questions. In his writings, Bruner suggests that learning is about participating in an experience "that makes the establishment of knowledge" possible (Bruner 1966, p. 72). For Bruner, "Knowing is a process, not a product" (ibid., p. 72).

The idea of experience as essential to learning reflects typical childhood behaviors. This is easily seen in the curiosity of a small child exploring objects in her environment using every sense – sight, sound, taste, touch, and smell. Theorists in the constructivist camp are united in their belief that young children actively engage in learning through sensory experiences and social interactions.

Theme II: Play

Play is declared essential to learning for children and described by Piaget ([1951] 1962) "as a child's work." It is a concept that is highly valued by experts in the field of child psychology and development, but is often given less respect by those outside of these fields. Play has many forms and contributes to learning in diverse ways. It can be formal or informal, structured or spontaneous, independent or interactive. Understanding play as a vehicle for learning offers museum practitioners opportunities to engage young children in meaningful ways with collections.

From Vygotsky to Piaget, play is foremost in defining how children make sense of their world. In play, children imitate everyday experiences by taking on roles to make meaning of what they see and experience. They extend ideas to express new thoughts through imaginative play scenarios. They create experiences using symbols to represent things in the real world, a stick for a horse, a block for a cell phone, a box for a car. Play allows children

> [to] move from the reality of the here and now – the world that children experience through their senses – to the imagined world of what might be … from the actual to the possible, from the concrete to the abstract, from the *what is* to answering the question *what if*, and acting in ways that suggest *as if*.
> Krakowski 2012, pp. 55–56

Theme III: Ways of Knowing

Ways of knowing is a theme that represents aptitudes or approaches to learning and acknowledges that people understand their world in diverse ways. Howard Gardner (1943–) advanced this idea in his *Frames of Mind: The Theory of Multiple Intelligences* (Gardner 1983), challenging the status quo of defining intelligence primarily by linguistic and mathematical capabilities. Gardner argues that individuals have different strengths and capacities to process experiences as well as construct meaning, initially identifying seven intelligences in his theory:

1. logical-mathematical
2. spatial

3. linguistic
4. bodily-kinesthetic
5. musical
6. interpersonal
7. intrapersonal.

He later contemplated naturalistic and existentialist as intelligences to consider.

Gardner's theory expanded thinking about ways of knowing with a special nod to the arts. Advocacy for dance, music, theater, and visual arts also came from within the arts community through the leadership of Elliott Eisner (1933–2014). For Eisner, aesthetics are a reflection of the heart which in turn brings with it "experiential rewards of taking the journey" (Eisner 1985, p. 35).

Theme IV: Motivation and Learning

Motivation is yet another topic examined by theorists in an attempt to understand learning. A common thread that emerges is personal interest as a driving force in the learning process. Dewey (1897, p. 15) stated "Only through the continual and sympathetic observation of childhood interests can the adult enter a child's life and see what it is ready for, and upon what material it could work most readily and fruitfully." Similarly, Bruner (1960) noted the significance of "arousing the child's interest in the world of ideas" (p. 31).

Abraham Maslow (1908–1970) envisioned motivation in the context of personal need or fulfillment and noted that physiological needs, safety, and belonging must be addressed before an individual can attend to higher states of achievement and fulfillment. Maslow's model acknowledges external factors as influential in learning.

Mihaly Csikszentmihalyi (1934–) suggests that motivation can be defined by its origins; intrinsic motivation stems from internal desire or interest whereas extrinsic motivation is driven by external rewards or circumstances. Csikszentmihalyi and Hermanson (1999) examined motivation in the context of museums and suggested "the museum exhibit must capture the visitors' curiosity" as the "first step in the process of intrinsically motivated learning" (p. 153), followed by sustaining interest.

Csikszentmihalyi added to the learning lexicon with the term *flow*, an idea closely linked to motivation. The concept of *flow* refers to an individual's actions at a very high level of competence, almost without thought, due to highly developed skills. Accomplished dancers and musicians or highly skilled athletes fall into this category. And while peak performances by Yo-Yo Ma or Michael Jordan could be explained by the term *flow*, the concept is also relevant when thinking about other types of activities. A young child painting at an easel, lost in the process, or a child building with blocks, absorbed in the activity to the exclusion of all else, are also examples of flow. The intrinsic nature of flow seems to be more highly valued in learning when compared to external rewards associated with extrinsic motivation.

The Study of Theory

The study of theory is important for museum professionals and helps to build a framework for understanding how children learn. But it is also important to remember that most museum professionals have informal knowledge of children which comes from personal observations and past experiences with little ones, through interactions with family members and children in the community. In fact, most people are able to describe typical behaviors associated with children, which contributes to an individual's intuitive understanding of the audience. But a deeper understanding is essential. It takes far more than this brief introduction to educational theory to be prepared, but, hopefully, it opens the door and encourages future study.

Conclusion

Museums are amazing places to inspire, engage, and encourage young children as learners. Through this overview of the history of children and museums, we see the immense changes that occurred and can build on the accomplishments from the past. By comparing today's offerings and opportunities for kindergartners, preschoolers, and toddlers with experiences of yesterday, we see that early learning is respected more today than at any other time.

This is a moment of opportunity for museum professionals to advance the early learning agenda for the benefit of young children and families, and to delve more deeply into ideas related to museums and children, particularly the role of objects in learning and the ways that young children are inspired by things that surround them.

This book encourages museum professionals, early childhood educators, parents, and advocates for the young to examine the relationship between children and objects, looking to the past for examples of object lessons, considering practices of today, and imagining the future as a place where technology is changing how people interact with their environment.

2

THE MUSEUM OBJECT: A STORY OF CHANGE

> The union of people's experiences and the unique characteristics of objects forms the foundation of something far greater than the sum of its parts.
>
> Elizabeth Wood and Kiersten F. Latham, 2014

Introduction

The story of museums is inextricably linked to the idea of collecting and the primacy of objects in the lives of people, a fact easily documented across time and culture. Early museums began as repositories for objects, studied by experts and displayed for the public as a method of disseminating knowledge. The idea that education is integral to museums is broadly accepted by society and captured in the mission statements of institutions as exemplified by the well-known phrase tied to the Smithsonian Institution, "the increase and diffusion of knowledge," words suggesting that knowledge is singular or finite as a truth shared by all, with museums as a conduit for educating visitors. Only in the latter part of the twentieth century were challenges to this notion raised in the context of museum learning and emphasis shifted from the object as a representation of truth to a framework that includes the visitor's personal experience. It is this move from an object-centric perspective to visitor-centered experience in galleries that illustrates the changing nature and understanding of objects in collecting museums. The words of Elizabeth Wood and Kiersten Latham underscore this critical relationship connecting experience to objects, highlighting current thinking in museums.

As fundamental beliefs about objects in more traditional museums evolved, the role of objects in children's museums also took on new meaning over time. The 1899 opening of the Brooklyn Children's Museum (BCM) offered child-friendly galleries where objects were carefully displayed for children to view. Early children's museums retained a commitment to collections, similar to traditional museums, but recreated galleries to be more child-friendly with lower cases and fewer labels and filled with specimens representing the natural world, an interest typically associated with children.

Children's museums of the early twentieth century also introduced young visitors to collections through a new and exciting approach that included handling of objects. In 1902, Anna Billings Gallup, curatorial assistant for the Brooklyn Children's Museum, brought innovative thinking into the museum galleries by offering tactile experiences for young visitors, certainly a significant departure from more traditional museum practices. In Gallup's words, "Brooklyn children flocked into their own museum to observe, to handle, and to discuss their new found treasures" (Hein 2012, p. 84).

Collections continued to be defining features for most children's museums until the 1960s' groundbreaking work of Frank Oppenheimer at the Exploratorium and Michael Spock of the Boston Children's Museum changed the landscape of museums forever, rejuvenating the children's museum movement following a period of dormancy.

By 1975, thirty-eight children's museums had opened their doors with exhibitions and experiences crafted for the younger visitor (ACM 2017), marking the beginning of a new trend across America that built on the innovations of Oppenheimer and Spock and paid homage to the developmental learning style of the young. It was the beginning of explosive growth for children's museums. With these changes, the role of the object morphed, giving way to ideas of play and interactive learning. History documents these changes and brings to light the evolving role and understanding of objects across museums, a concept that can be seen in traditional collecting institutions as well as in galleries created specifically for children.

The Ubiquitous Nature of Objects

Objects have long been associated with the idea of museums, from the earliest informal displays in the homes of the wealthy to twenty-first-century collections found in diverse museums representing myriad perspectives. The idea that objects hold a significant place in museums is seemingly obvious, yet important to acknowledge as a foundational tenet that is deeply embedded in the historical narrative of the museum. In today's world, objects remain important to the mission and vision of most museums even though the manner in which objects are perceived is changing.

Museum collections, comprising carefully selected objects that reflect the mission of the institution and in many cases its cultural values, illustrate the complexity of the world and the ingenuity of mankind, from rare scientific specimens to cultural artifacts and works of art. Objects capture the imagination of the curious public, provide a window into the past, open doors to understanding cultural traditions and practices from around the world, represent stories that range from the familiar to the unfamiliar, and are remarkable in their ability to evoke emotional response.

There is little doubt that objects play an important role in our everyday lives as well as in museums.

Objects are ubiquitous, a part of everyday life experience with some regarded as valuable and others seemingly insignificant. At times, objects fade into the landscape of life, gaining prominence only when the item serves a specific purpose or receives attention for some other reason, possibly as simple as being a source of curiosity which leads to a desire to explore and know more. Objects are intricately entwined in our lives; they hold memories, represent interests, trigger emotion, and define our personal history. Any one of these connections can serve as the beginning point for a collector.

Objects vary from natural specimens to manmade artifacts, many of which capture attention or provoke curiosity. Interest in things that make up the natural environment, from rocks and gems to nests and feathers, often begins at an early age and continues throughout life. Children enamored with the natural world at an early age are likely to be the entomologists, ornithologists, and paleontologists of the future.

Amazing specimens created by nature are not the only inspiration for collectors. Cultural artifacts represent a very different aspect of the world and serve as a source of intrigue for many. Manmade objects represent people and places around the globe throughout the history of mankind; they can be traced back in time to discoveries of early artifacts, such as stone tools which are believed to be more than 2.6 million years old (Smithsonian Institution National Museum of Natural History 2016). Although not nearly as old as the original stone tools, prehistoric cave paintings also provide evidence of objects used as tools by early man.

Many of the first manmade objects were utilitarian in nature, but over time, they moved beyond pure necessity and reflected experimentation with materials as well as refinement of skills or craftsmanship, leading to innovation with groups seeking "their own cultural identity" and adopting "their own way of making things" (ibid.). For example, clay containers initially served a specific function, but over time were created not only for purpose but with an eye toward innovative design imagined by the artist. The identity of the object was broadening to reflect the vision of the craftsman and the culture of the time. An example of this shift from purpose to artistry and innovation is seen in the work of George Ohr, the self-proclaimed Mad Potter from Biloxi, in Mississippi. Recognized as the "first of the artist-potters in the United States, and arguably the finest" (Black 2009, p. 18), Ohr began his career "with practical consumer items like coffee mugs, flower pots, flue pipes, and pitchers," but later privileged technique, whimsy, and imagination in his creations over function (ibid., p. 18).

In today's world, the number of personal encounters with objects is remarkable, almost beyond comprehension, with any one object available in a wide variety of choices. The richness and complexity of objects that make up the twenty-first-century world are seemingly endless. Even as the role of objects changes in people's lives and in America's museums, it is impossible to think about the human experience without considering the place or value of the object.

Objects in Museums: A Changing Perspective

Humankind's ingenuity is readily evident in the vast array of artifacts created by people across time and place, a fact easily recognized by the diversity of museum collections. In the twenty-first century, thinking about museums evolved from perceiving these institutions as places for warehousing treasures, or, in the case of the Smithsonian Institution, as the nation's attic, to understanding that museums were no longer simply a "repository for priceless and not-so-priceless objects" (Schwarzer 2006, p. 1). The new vision is defined by a more complex approach to how objects are perceived and understood. In *Riches, Rivals, & Radicals: 100 Years of Museums in America*, author Marjorie Schwarzer describes that change. "Once the authoritative interpreter of priceless objects, it [the museum] now also acknowledges the many interpretations of its visitors" (ibid., p. 2). This shift, from the belief that knowledge resides within the object, going beyond certifiable provenance and history, to the conviction that meaning is constructed and exists uniquely for each person, is playing out in western museums today and being considered as a possibility by many educators and museum professionals from around the world.

The origins of this change in perspective took root in the experiential or participatory movement started in the 1960s (H. Hein 2011) and gathered momentum in light of the 1992 publication of *Excellence and Equity: Education and the Public Dimension of Museums* (AAM 1992) and the mandate to "place education in the broadest sense of the word – at the center of their public service role" (p. 8). The Museum Task Force crafting this forward-thinking public statement suggested a new balance and partnership among colleagues representing collecting, preservation, research, and education to diminish tensions of the past and consider the role of the visitor as interpreter. The initiative highlighting education and diversity, promised change for exhibition design and content as well as for the visitor's role in constructing meaning.

Excellence and Equity's unequivocal directive to the museum community at large sought new emphasis on education, thereby recognizing the significance of the visitor and acknowledging that "museums have the potential to be enriched and enlivened by the nation's diversity" (ibid.). The value of visitor perspective addressed by this groundbreaking decree was further supported and broadened in scope by a growing interest in constructivist learning theory, beliefs brought to fore in museum practices of the 1990s by George E. Hein, a leading authority in the museum sector, but also by others in the broader education field.

Hein's rigorous examination of learning theory and its application in museums referenced a range of perspectives held by well-known philosophers of the nineteenth and twentieth centuries, challenging educators to re-evaluate their thinking about the museum experience. In Hein's (1998) publication, *Learning in the Museum*, he concludes "that visitors can best learn when knowledge is actively constructed in their own minds, in exhibitions which are physically, socially, and intellectually accessible to every single visitor" (back cover).

In the intervening years from the 1990s until now, the transition from an object-centered culture in museums to a visitor perspective was not always smooth, and at times, slow to gain acceptance, particularly among smaller institutions, yet evolve it did. Greater understanding came from the work of museum practitioners eager to examine theory and practice to advance thinking in the field. *From Periphery to Center: Art Museum Education in the 21st Century* (Mayer 2007) is one example illustrating the desire to study underlying theory and explore gallery techniques with a broad range of authors. In one of the text's essays, Melinda Mayer suggested that conversation among visitors and with museum educators is essential to meaning making and should be the norm rather than the exception in art galleries. She noted that the norm since the 1980s "reflects an increasing balance between careful attention to objects and audience," but encouraged even greater emphasis on conversation and interaction in the galleries, suggesting that "more memorable relationships with works of art" may occur when the focus is on the visitor, rather than the object (ibid., p. 189). This transition from an object-centered culture in museums to a visitor perspective, while incomplete, continues to be a topic of interest, debate, and discussion.

Within the museum field, differing points of view with analysis of contrasting ideas appeared in professional journals, an outcome of debates among museum colleagues. For some, the tension between protecting precious objects and serving the public was a critical topic of conversation, certainly a point of interest for Elisabeth Sommer, guest editor for the *Journal of Museum Education* in 2011. In the Introduction, she acknowledges that "even attempts to follow the mandate [*Excellence and Equity*] to emphasize education and the visitor experience frequently fall short of truly breaking the traditional mold" (Sommer 2011, p. 130), at least in the traditional models represented in history and art museums. Sommer notes that visitor experience is an integral aspect of science and children's museums where there is greater opportunity for more hands-on experience by visitors, in contrast with other types of museums.

The practice of interactive or hands-on experience is a topic addressed by Hilde Hein in the *Journal of Museum Education* in 2011. She offers an article providing "a theoretical framework for thinking about the role of objects in the 21st century museum" (H. Hein 2011) and suggests that the move by museums to focus on the experience of visitors rather than the object as a means to "simply preserve precious artifacts, impart knowledge, and transmit cultural heritage" is indeed the result of emphasizing "active engagement, including 'hands-on' operation that encourages learners to make knowledge their own rather than submitting passively to its imposition" (p. 181). She further speculates that this path "permitted a plurality of points of view to flourish and respected people's capacity to reach their own conclusions" (ibid., p. 181), a view which continues to receive attention in museums today.

As Hilde Hein suggests, there is widespread recognition that a given object will be perceived in different ways, allowing for "a plurality of points of view" (p. 181), due to factors ranging from the visitor's background knowledge, personal experience, interest, and culture. For example, a jeweled brooch in the shape of a crane may be appreciated by some for its aesthetic beauty or the choice of precious gems while others see the artifact for its symbolism in Chinese culture. Still another individual is reminded of a jeweled family heirloom passed from one generation to the next while someone else is less enamored by the object, preferring the simplicity of gold or silver without gems. A visitor's personal preferences and background play a vital role in the experience with the object, a fact that does nothing to change the history or provenance of the artifact itself, but rather contributes to the emotional response elicited and the meaning constructed as part of the experience. This is the visitor's story.

Understanding the role of the object continues to be a topic of contemplation, research, and conversation in the museum field in 2017 and builds on the academic offerings of recent years. *The Objects of Experience: Transforming Visitor-Object Encounters in Museums*, a text by Elizabeth Wood and Kiersten Latham (2014), is one such work that offers insight into the role of objects in the visitor experience. Their work emphasizes the museum's responsibility to create "compelling encounters with objects" by designing museum experiences with the understanding that "object meanings are not static records or entries in a database: rather they are the infinite meanings brought to each object by everyone who has ever encountered it, before or during its life in a museum" (ibid., p. 163). The authors make a case for new directions in museum practice by encouraging museum practitioners to design gallery experiences and programs around the belief that visitor encounters with objects are unique for each individual, but also with recognition that "these encounters do follow patterns that are just as useful for successful and fulfilling planning in museums" (ibid., p. 21). The authors encourage deeper exploration of human connections to objects in the twenty-first-century museum.

In 2017, the transition could well be defined as a blurring of lines between the old and the new, a place without total clarity regarding the balance between context and meaning embedded in the object and the influence of the visitor in the interpretative process. *What role do curatorial experts play in museums? Is every object open to interpretation by visitors or are there certain types of objects where this new emphasis on the visitor is less fitting? What does this mean for interpretative techniques such as audio tours or lectures? How will exhibit design change as museum professionals consider the visitor's point of view?* Although the significance of the visitor's perspective is given greater consideration in today's museum, there are still many institutions where practice and philosophical theories of the day are not aligned and where questions still exist about the balance between the object and the visitor. Without doubt, this discussion deserves further consideration.

The discussion about interpretation of objects is also changing the role of educators in museums. They are seeking a greater voice in the development of their institution's exhibitions and programs as equal partners with curators and exhibition designers rather than an afterthought. The good news is that there are examples of collaboration in exhibition planning in many museums, yet there are still remnants of past practice where a hierarchy exists with researchers as decision-makers and educators being marginalized.

In the museum field at large, education is gaining support and recognition for its vital role in interpretation that challenges the status of the past, certainly when compared to practices in the twentieth century. For many practitioners, there is still a concern that education has not gained the universal respect it deserves. In

Sommer's words, "We should not be satisfied, however, until the 1992 mandate given in *Excellence and Equity* is the rule from the Smithsonian to the county historical societies" (Sommer 2011, p. 131). This emphasis on education as a defining role within museums, and with the privileges that it deserves, is a goal that museum educators continue to pursue.

The Role of Objects in Museums: Views from Traditional Museums and Children's Museums

Perspectives from the Field: Questionnaires, Interviews, and Responses to an On-Line Museum Forum

As an author and practitioner in the museum field, I believe that perspectives from the field are essential for understanding beliefs and practices in museums. To that end, I created a questionnaire for colleagues, following up with informal interviews in some cases, to gather perspectives representing a broad range of museums and widened the scope of participants through the use of Open Forum, AAM's on-line discussion platform. Responses from each of these sources are integrated into the following section. Research studies and academic literature from books and articles represent yet another important perspective that offers insight into understanding the role of objects in children's learning in different types of museums.

Objects are, and have been for centuries, associated with the idea of museums. With the diverse nature of museums from the formal, collecting institutions to the more informal, play-based organizations, it is not surprising to learn that professionals in the field define objects in different ways and hold varying viewpoints about the place of objects in learning and their role in museums. To gain insight into practices that support children's learning, in museums as well as other environments, several questions frame the analysis:

- What role do objects play in children's learning?
- What does this look like in a traditional collecting museum?
- How does this differ in a children's museum environment?
- What is the value of the authentic object for children's learning?
- Why are objects powerful tools for children's learning?

These questions, and others, are the starting point for understanding diversity of thought within the field and recognition of opportunities for collaborative learning as it relates to children.

Perspectives on Objects and Collections in Traditional Museums

Traditional museums in the twenty-first century retain many features of collecting museums of the past while also adapting to new ways of thinking about objects and visitors. For children, a visit to a traditional museum revolves around the awe and excitement of seeing things that one would otherwise not encounter in everyday experience, ranging from dinosaur fossils and skeletons in natural history museums to musical instruments made from dried gourds and other natural materials in cultural institutions. Children's interests and curiosities are driving forces in how the museum experience is shaped. Objects in exhibitions as well as those available for hands-on experiences are critical elements of the traditional museum and contribute to meaning making in the gallery, for young and old alike.

Scott Paris (2002), author of *Perspectives on Object-Centered Learning in Museums*, presents a starting point for thinking about the specific nature of objects and the opportunities they offer:

> Being in the presence of an original object can be uplifting. Talking about your own reactions to objects can be edifying. Responding to an object can deepen the experience. Authentic, unique, and first-hand experiences with objects stimulate curiosity, exploration, and emotions. These are the features of an object-based epistemology that stands in contrast to the traditional methods of learning through text and discourse.
>
> *p. xvi*

Paris recognizes the power of "being in the presence of an original object" (ibid., p. xvi), what children talk about as the real thing. Children want to *see with their own eyes* and are somehow unconvinced until they see the real thing. In fact, most preschoolers visiting museums do not hesitate to ask the question "Is it real?" Is that dinosaur bone real? Are those shark teeth real? Even though children may lack a sophisticated understanding of what the term *real* means, there is still a sense that something is special or unique when it's real, and this understanding changes the dynamic of the experience dramatically, increasing a child's interest and attention. A child's desire for the real thing mirrors Paris' reference to original objects.

Paris also suggests that first-hand experiences with authentic objects stimulate curiosity. Young children, as naturally curious beings, are attracted to a wide variety of artifacts in museums from a nineteenth-century fire pumper at the National Museum of American History to an early twentieth-century kettle-shaped drum from Ghana at the Metropolitan Museum of Art. The initial attraction may be the novelty of each artifact, yet these objects also retain familiar features that allow children to make meaningful connections.

Curiosity is a driving force that underlies the behavior of young children and stimulates a desire to know and witness the real over the reproduction. Allison Wickens, Vice President for Education at Mount Vernon, makes this point, noting that "a plastic fire hat and a real firefighter's helmet are different experiences for a young child" with the latter of greater value "for the connections it can build to the real world" (Wickens, questionnaire, 2017). Wickens believes that especially in history museums and historic sites, "the connection to people of the past is so much better illustrated with artifacts than conceptual descriptions of people who lived long ago" (Wickens, questionnaire, 2017). A child's interests are equally powerful.

What cannot be overlooked in this conversation is the value of the concrete object in learning, a sentiment that Paris alludes to when describing the benefits of an object-based epistemology. Objects are a focal point of museums, past and present, as a source of knowledge and study by researchers, but equally important for their ability to inspire, intrigue, and engage the public when displayed thoughtfully.

A dominant feature of children's learning is the natural inclination to integrate experiences and construct meaning about the world through the senses of sight, sound, taste, touch, and smell. Children thrive in environments where they are able to actively engage with objects. They are curious about what they see and excited by the knowledge that an artifact or specimen is real. They seek opportunities to explore through their senses. In the twenty-first-century museum, visitors benefit from a broad range of experiences that heighten learning by engaging multiple senses. For example, a family looks closely at a collection of Sweetgrass Baskets, a traditional art form of basket making brought to America by enslaved peoples in the seventeenth century. The children discover more about the artifacts through a hands-on gallery activity where visitors examine the texture of various fibers and then experiment with weaving techniques similar to those used to create the artifacts on display. A brief video shows women making sweetgrass baskets and provides insight as well as context for the process. A range of objects, from the accessioned artifacts to the everyday materials such as plant fibers, contribute to visitors' ability to construct meaning.

In an ideal world, there would be some form of sensory experience in traditional museums, not touching the artifact itself, but rather an opportunity to expand children's experience through other sensory encounters such as listening to the sounds made by the pumper truck or actively beating a reproduction of a drum similar to the exhibit artifact. Although sensory experiences offer multiple entry points for connecting to artifacts in the collection, it is important to realize that the richness of the visual experience, in and of itself, has merit for children's learning.

Early childhood expert, Dr. Alyson Williams, supports the premise that traditional exhibitions offer opportunities for learning even without tactile or multisensory experiences and suggests that the organization of displayed objects conveys meaning to young children. In a natural history museum "They [the children] are learning methods of classification – here are the butterflies and there are the beetles – an essential early mathematical and scientific thinking skill" (Williams, questionnaire, 2017). In Williams' example, children develop observation skills as they look closely to discern the differences among beetles while also noting similarities. Attention to detail cannot be underestimated in its value. Again, while seemingly simple, children hone their skills in looking closely and learn to compare objects, building important skills essential to future learning.

As suggested by Williams, sight is a powerful tool for learning. Seeing a turtle shell or a peddler's cart from the early days of America are museum objects with potential appeal for children. The visual experience is often the beginning of the learning process for museum visitors and the basis for understanding the rudimentary physical properties of the artifact or specimen.

As Paris (2002) suggests, "being in the presence of an original object" has the power to "deepen the experience … to stimulate curiosity, exploration, and emotions" (p. xvi). This belief was echoed by many questionnaire participants. Barbara Franco, an independent scholar and museum consultant, related her personal experience with the exhibition *Childhood Treasures* (in the National Heritage Museum, Lexington, MA), reminiscing about the emotional ties formed between children and objects. In designing the exhibition, Franco and her colleagues researched childhood treasures and stories, finding that most children possess "treasure boxes and the bits and pieces that are important to them" (Franco, questionnaire, 2017) and that the memories and emotions remain intact throughout adulthood. In many cases, the objects of interest at an early age were indicative of future life events. "A man who collected toy trains worked for the railroad his entire life. A toy ship … belonged to a man who later became an admiral in the Navy" (Franco, questionnaire, 2017). Franco remembers the "remarkable stories of how objects figured in these childhoods" (Franco, questionnaire, 2017) and also the emotional reactions of adult visitors when they encountered objects in the exhibition that reminded them of personal items from their youth. Meaning was constructed by each individual in response to an object.

In *The Participatory Museum*, Nina Simon (2010) draws attention to objects and their social implications as she discusses opportunities to shift visitor experience from the passive to the active, an approach that certainly aligns with children's needs and desires. Simon suggests that the social object is one that "consistently draws a talkative crowd" (ibid., p. 129) and is best described as "personal, active, provocative, and relational" (ibid., p. 129), seeing each of these descriptors as a point of entry for conversation among visitors.

Social objects exist in every museum and are a useful approach for engaging children as well as adults. At the National Museum of American History in Washington, DC, a display of old-fashioned, metal lunch boxes from the mid-twentieth century evokes memories from visitors of a certain age, but also opens conversations that are cross-generational with comparisons to lunch box characters of today. The objects are so powerful in eliciting memories and emotion that people are likely to share personal stories with others who might have similar experiences. Children are less reticent in their interactions with others outside the family group, and in many cases, will eagerly share their feelings about a specific object that has relevance in their lives. A collection of unique shells from Sanibel Island is likely to provoke conversation after a child's trip to the beach. Objects have potential to create common ground for conversation or open dialogue about shared experiences.

The twenty-first-century museum is no longer exclusively about objects on pedestals, protected by glass. Many exhibitions engage the senses in ways unimagined fifty years ago and welcome diverse perspectives in the topics addressed and audiences served. In this attempt to serve more diverse visitors, specifically young children, many traditional museums offer hands-on discovery spaces or other specially designed environments that accommodate early learners. For example, the

National Museum of American History in Washington, DC, opened Wegman's Wonderplace in 2015, a space catering to the under-six crowd by encouraging play, yet also displays authentic artifacts that appeal to young children. On its website, it states:

> Our youngest visitors will cook their way through a kid-size Julia Childs kitchen, find the owls hiding in the Smithsonian Castle, and captain a tugboat based on a model from our collections. Through playful activities and creative displays of treasured artifacts, young children will get to know the faces, places, and stories of our country in engaging and appropriate ways.

Play-based spaces in collecting museums exist in institutions of all types, from art and history museums to science and culture centers, and are sought-after experiences for many young families. They are founded on the premise that playful interactions connecting children with real objects inspire and motivate young museum-goers to venture beyond the play environment to find meaning in artifacts, specimens, or works of art displayed in the broader museum.

The traditional museum of today reflects a changing world, where objects and visitors are both valued for interpretation, and diversity is welcomed, including early learners. It is a place where a sense of wonder is the expectation and where objects inspire questions and conversations. It offers opportunities to "be in the presence of original objects" that "stir curiosity, exploration, and emotion" (Paris 2002, p. xvi).

Perspectives on Objects and Collections in Children's Museums

Children's museums are broad and varied, from the exclusively play-based experience to the science-driven program supporting a STEM (Science, Technology, Engineering, and Mathematics) initiative. In the twenty-first century, the idea of play is integrated into almost every genre of children's museum and part of a philosophy that builds on educational theory of child development.

The Association of Children's Museums (ACM) advances the idea of play across member institutions and touts exploration as part of the play-based experience. Words like *interactive, hands-on,* and *touch* are used by ACM to describe activities in children's museums and are linked to the play-based experience, but also have meaning for the discussion of object-based learning. *About Children's Museums* on ACM's website (ACM 2017) describes this play-based emphasis in museums:

> Peek inside a children's museum and you'll see babies and toddlers touching a variety of textures, stacking blocks, crawling through a tunnel, or blowing bubbles. Take another look inside a children's museum to see boys and girls enter a 19th century ship where they hoist a net full of fish, take part in a fishing derby, raise and lower sails and semaphore flags, all the while building

an understanding of maritime history. Say adios to rigid rules: at a children's museum the general rule is: Please Touch!

Objects are certainly part of the children's museum experience, as evidenced by the ACM description, where they are viewed primarily as props that encourage imagination in support of child-driven, play activities, a context that differs from that of a more traditional museum. Interaction with objects from blocks and bubbles to the nineteenth-century ship with flags and sails reflects an object-centric environment, in this case, objects that serve as props for inviting play.

ACM more clearly defines objects in the Association's Standards for Professional Practice in Children's Museums (ibid.), a definition that can be viewed in the context of learning and exploration:

> As defined for children's museums, objects primarily serve as tools to motivate learning and address the developmental needs of children. They are instruments for carrying out the children's museum's educational objectives, and reflect these purposes. The mode of presentation is substantially interactive and contextual. Objects may not necessarily have intrinsic value to science, history, art, or culture, and can include constructed activity pieces and exhibit components.

This Standard aligns with the play-based practice typical of children's museums of the past fifty years and also stands in contrast to the more traditional collecting museum. Objects that are part of exhibitions and programming, from props to real-world things, are the collection of the museum and offer opportunities to engage children through their senses and allow for independent and shared exploration.

Props are vital components of most play-based experiences. For example, at the Miami Children's Museum in Florida, visitors are encouraged to learn about the cruise industry by stepping aboard a recreated version of a Carnival cruise ship where children are challenged to take part in a "limbo competition or even become a cruise entertainer for a day" (Miami Children's Museum 2017). The play space engages children in activities reminiscent of the work of crew members as well as the leisure activities of passengers, all guiding young museum visitors to discover what life might be like aboard a cruise ship. The Children's Museum of Denver in Colorado offers a variety of experiences, many of which are play-based, where pretend play is encouraged as children step into social roles in veterinary clinics, dental offices, fire stations, markets and more. In *My Market*, toddlers and preschoolers enjoy weighing and measuring produce, check out customers at the cash register, and prepare meals in a 1940s kitchen. Objects in most of these play-based experiences are props, designed to look similar to the real thing, but more durable for children's constant handling and play.

In these instances, objects as props support play and learning, but clearly are different in nature when compared to objects accessioned in collecting museums. In an interview with ACM's Executive Director, Laura Huerta Migus, she gives clarity to the role of objects in children's museums and frames the conversation by defining objects as representational, re-created to reflect real-world objects and scenarios for children's consumption through play and exploration (Migus, interview, 2017). She suggests that by scaling down the real world for children's play, children gain access to things that are typically off-limits in the real world. Beyond simply re-creating objects that reflect a child's world, Migus advances the idea that objects are tools for learning or mechanisms that are a means to an end. This is reflected in maker spaces in children's museums as well as in other types of exhibitions.

When comparing objects in traditional museums with those in children's museums, Migus acknowledges that the significance or inherent value of objects collected and preserved by traditional museums is different from the value of objects typically found in play-based spaces. She points out that a concept such as authenticity, for example, crosses boundaries between traditional and play-based organizations, but that authenticity, and its significance, are more highly valued by traditional museums. Based on changing views among educators in children's museums, Migus reports renewed emphasis on real-world objects, particularly in cultural exhibitions such as *Hello from Japan!*, but also sees this commitment in the design of immersive exhibitions that reflect natural environments.

This attempt to incorporate authentic objects into exhibitions is borne out in places like Hawaii Children's Discovery Center where authentic objects are integrated into a variety of programs and exhibitions. Board Chair, Loretta Yajima, describes one such program, *Living Legacies*, and the inclusion of "authentic objects from different countries to create a sense of history and culture" (Yajima, questionnaire, 2017). According to Yajima, objects from "China, Portugal, Japan, Korea, and the Philippines" are used to show "the history of the plantation workers, to know where they came from" (Yajima, questionnaire, 2017). She suggests that "the role of objects is to pique a child's curiosity … and make connections to the real world," and acknowledges that children react differently to objects that are real and describes this as "a shift in how they think" (Yajima, questionnaire, 2017), which adds value to the experience, and ultimately, children's memories of the event.

In a recent interview, Dr. Elee Wood, co-author of *The Objects of Experience: Transforming Visitor Encounters in Museums* (Wood and Latham 2014) suggests that objects, from the mundane to the museum-worthy, offer opportunities for learning. She further indicates her belief that in a digital world, authentic objects serve a vital role and offer learners an opportunity to test or verify what they see or experience in other ways. In thinking about children's museums, Wood raises the idea of context and suggests that situating an object in a meaningful environment increases a child's ability to make meaning. From her perspective, children's museums provide context that is sometimes missing in traditional exhibitions. This too is changing in the twenty-first century where many traditional exhibitions afford visitors broader context and increased opportunities for understanding objects.

Interest in authentic objects is gaining renewed interest in children's museums today. Historically, children's museums were opened as collecting institutions, similar to more traditional museums, yet with a distinctive perspective honoring children as unique learners needing a different type of experience with objects.

The commitment to collections and the belief in the value of authentic objects continues today in the work of the Brooklyn Children's Museum (BCM), the first museum of its kind. More than 100 years after its opening in 1899, the website states: "Brooklyn Children's Museum remains one of only a handful of children's museums with a permanent collection, which today includes nearly 30,000 cultural and natural science objects that are utilized in programs, exhibitions, and media." According to Petrushka Bazin Larsen, Vice President of Programs and Education, authentic objects connect children to the real world, past and present, and in her words "bring our exhibits to life" (Larsen, questionnaire, 2017). The Museum's dedication to hands-on, sensory learning is also on display in exhibitions like Brooklyn Block Lab and Neighborhood Nature, spaces that encourage investigation as well as role play. Artifacts from the collection enrich children's experiences and support the Institution's beliefs that "the Collection is not valuable unless it is in the hands of children" (Calleri, email, February 2, 2017).

The Boston Children's Museum (1913) followed in the footsteps of the Brooklyn Children's Museum and is also one of only a few children's museums today maintaining a permanent collection. The organization is committed to interactive learning and play, a movement from the 1960s credited to its then museum's director, Michael Spock. In *Boston Stories* (Spock 2013), Spock writes of the heady time when organizational leaders were "looking for ways to seize control and transform the sleepy, almost 50-year organization into an experimental platform for innovation in informal education" (ibid., p. 24). To reflect changing beliefs, "Do Not Touch" signs were removed from the learning environment and a visitor-centered philosophy was adopted.

Another influential leader heralded for its historic permanent collection is the Children's Museum of Indianapolis (1925), yet also celebrated for its child-centered play spaces and experiences. The Museum's interest in objects is captured in a description on its website:

> Objects from the past aren't just something to admire. They carry stories – powerful stories that can inspire, teach, and even change lives. Over 120,000 artifacts and specimens are housed within The Children's Museum, helping to bring the museum to life for visitors in extraordinary ways. With a rich collection history of more than 80 years, the museum has been using objects to inspire imaginations and connect generations for decades.
>
> *The Children's Museum of Indianapolis website 2017*

According to Susan Foutz, Director of Research and Evaluation at The Children's Museum of Indianapolis, there is value in "seeing the real thing" and integrating objects that tell important stories is key to fulfilling the museum's mission (Foutz, interview, 2017). "Objects spark conversation" (Foutz, interview, 2017) and serve as a catalyst for intergenerational dialogue.

In the current exhibition, *The Galleries for American Arts and Popular Culture*, comic books with familiar characters that span decades generate conversation among grandparents and grandchildren (Figure 2.1). If comic books don't grab a child's attention, then maybe one of the other collections – Beanie Babies, cowboy boots, Star Wars action figures or Batman toys and movie props – will do the trick.

In other areas of the Museum, objects from the permanent collection are integrated into the exhibition space where hands-on experience is the norm. In *The Music Studio*, children explore sound as they play authentic instruments from around the world. Although the instruments handled by visitors are authentic, they are not part of the Museum's collection. In *The Art Studio*, paintings and sculptures from world-acclaimed artists, including Hunt Slonem, inspire budding artists to create personal masterpieces using a variety of art techniques from print making to collage. Children learn about their world through interaction with real objects in an environment that sees play as natural and worthwhile.

Although the value of authentic objects is gaining attention from professionals in the field, there are many children's museums without permanent collections, some by choice and others due to lack of resources of funding or space. As noted earlier, children's museums are broad and varied, and each needs to be respected for its educational philosophy and specific mission which may or may not include a collection.

FIGURE 2.1 The Children's Museum of Indianapolis. Family looking at the Max Simon comic book collection in the Galleries for American Arts and Popular Culture

Conclusion

Objects play an important part in children's learning, even though the way in which objects are perceived may differ among professionals representing different types of museums. By looking closely at the responses to questionnaires, listening to the perspectives voiced in interviews, and reviewing professional publications, there is an opportunity to identify similarities and differences in values, beliefs, and practices when comparing traditional museums with children's museums.

Traditional museums and children's museums share several beliefs and practices related to objects: (1) objects are important in children's learning; (2) objects offer opportunities to tell important stories; (3) objects inspire, ignite curiosity, and evoke emotion; and (4) objects are important due to their tangible nature and offer unique opportunities for tactile, sensory exploration and meaning making.

Objects, while important in traditional museums and children's museums, are not necessarily understood as serving the same purpose. In the traditional museum, objects are collected for preservation and study with the idea that information gleaned from study will contribute to a broader body of knowledge. At the same time, artifacts and scientific specimens are displayed for public consumption and are integral elements of stories told through exhibitions. In children's museums, objects are regarded as tools for serving children and their families in learning.

This leads to another noteworthy point of separation which is in the manner of defining objects. Authenticity is at the core of this difference, with traditional museums placing a high value on the criteria as part of the process of collecting and preserving, and they judge authentic or original objects as having greater value. It is this social construct that traditional museums value in a way that differs from their counterparts in children's museums where every tangible thing is categorized as an object, regardless of its inherent value. The difference in perspective is not inconsequential, but rather represents two competing views that conform to different standards.

A final critical point of interest is the difference in audience served. Traditional museums are intended to serve a wide-ranging, diverse audience, broadening after the call to action prompted by *Excellence and Equity*, whereas children's museums are intentional in their focus on exhibition and program designs, themes, and practices tailored to children and their families. They are about audience. There certainly is an intersection of those being served by both museums, yet the experiences that are offered are unique to the institution and its philosophy.

This brief look at the role of objects in museums is enhanced when children's learning is examined in the context of cognitive theory (see Chapter 1). It is also important to remember that museums, whether traditional or play-based children's museums, are far from one-dimensional and often reflect features that cross boundaries from what might be expected. Although there are many nuanced differences appropriate for discussion, there are just as many commonalities that can contribute to building new partnerships among professionals that draw from traditional and children's museums. Further study is necessary to continue to build on the successes of the past and expand opportunities for children's learning that comes from sharing innovative practices.

3

THE OBJECT LESSON: A CLOSER LOOK AT ITS HISTORY AND DEVELOPMENT

> Objects can act as catalysts in the learning process itself: the material aspect, the "realness" of objects, enables the possibility of an arousal of interest or a focus of attention that is qualitatively different from the attention given to the written word.
> Eilean Hooper-Greenhill (1991), p. 98

Introduction

The term "object lesson" has a place in formal and informal learning environments and is a concept historically documented in the writings of early European educational theorists such as the seventeenth-century Moravian philosopher and educator, John Amos Comenius, Swiss pedagogue and social reformer, Johann Pestalozzi, and German educator and founder of the kindergarten, Friedrich Froebel. Education was forever changed by the work of these men and their belief in concrete objects as a way of learning. Author Maurice Walter Keatinge described their impact in the historical background of his 1896 translation, *The Great Didactic of Comenius* (p. 150):

> To Comenius' eternal credit be it that he was the first to realise that the object-lesson was the only way in which any impression could be made on the half-developed thinking powers of the child, that he practically anticipated Pestalozzi, and paved the way for Froebel.

The underlying premise of the object lesson draws on the belief that learning stems from concrete experience and that thought begins with sensation. Eilean Hooper-Greenhill draws on this belief and advances the idea of objects as catalysts for learning, recognizing the material nature and realness of objects as essential to learning which she notes is in sharp contrast with learning that relies solely on the written word. Early advocates espousing similar beliefs understood that nature affords meaningful opportunities for object-centered learning, and in recognition of that idea, constructed object lessons that centered on objects found in the natural world.

The term "object lesson" or the notion of teaching with objects is initially found in the context of schooling and teaching of literacy, yet also consistently appears in descriptions of museum experiences crafted for the public with particular prominence in the nineteenth century. It is an idea that reaches across the broader realm of education and learning theory, a concept that continues to be relevant today.

Context for Understanding the Object Lesson, Past and Present

Searching historical literature for the term "object lesson" offers a baseline for understanding the idea and its origins, but is not sufficient for more in-depth analysis. References to the term "object lesson" are found in a variety of contexts, past and present, but most frequently are associated with museums. To explore the concept, it is helpful to look at one or two current-day references as well as tangential concepts to gain appreciation for the phrase and examine its meaning and practice over time.

A recent reference is found at the Manchester Museum (at the University of Manchester in the UK) in the exhibition, *Object Lessons*, which offers the public insight into the vision of art connoisseur George Loudon's "intriguing collection of 19th century life science teaching objects" with an opportunity "to view the natural world through the eyes of a Victorian scientist" (Manchester Museum 2017). *Object Lessons* includes artifacts from 1843 Japanese teaching scrolls to papier-mâché flowers, and showcases a broad range of items that historically served an educational function but today are revered for their aesthetic beauty. This blend of past and present shines a light on the idea of object lessons and illustrates its place in the context of the museum, but also in the broader realm of education with the scientist's tools.

In the summer of 2014, the University of Virginia magazine focused on "telling the history of UVA one piece at a time," not in words, but through a collection of historical objects. The article, "Object Lesson," presents images of artifacts from the university's treasured collection that range from "a lock of Thomas Jefferson's hair … to the basketball net cut down just after the Cavaliers won the 2014 ACC Tournament" (*UVA Magazine* 2014). This approach to sharing stories in history begins with a small collection of artifacts, an idea relevant to museums, yet also commonplace outside of the museum grounds.

References to object lessons are also prominent in Christian communities and services. Through the use of everyday objects, children are introduced to Biblical lessons, religious beliefs, and shared community values. This approach recognizes the impact of tangible objects for demonstrating accepted principles of Christian living and provides an opportunity to understand more abstract concepts. In this particular example, the object lesson falls outside of the museum world and is intended to be educative in nature.

References to object lessons appear in different contexts, yet there is one common bond, the focus on concrete objects. To delve more deeply into the idea of object lessons or object-based learning, it is essential to examine theories that consider the role of the object in learning and to examine how that relates to human behavior. Why is the object critical to learning and how does it change the nature of the learning process?

Interest in this process of learning was a driving force for Comenius as he thought about children and effective strategies to engage them more fully. It was equally important to the attempts of highly regarded theorists, such as John Dewey, seeking insight into the human condition of learning and methods of absorbing information or constructing knowledge. Although a broad range of competing theories exist, a constructivist view espousing active, sensory learning offers an approach that closely intersects with concepts relevant to the object lesson.

Constructivist learning is based on the idea of experience as critical to learning and recognizes active engagement as an essential component of experience, the bedrock principles of this progressive model, yet also at the core of object lessons. Experience includes interaction with concrete things of the world and implies exploration that includes a variety of sensory modalities. The tangible nature of the object allows for active, sensory investigation as a means of learning. For this reason, a brief history of object lessons will include an overview of the concept and its educational theory and practice, but it will also include ideas reflecting similar values and features, notably progressive education and constructivist learning. It is difficult to think about one without the other.

The Object Lesson in Educational Theory and Practice

Challenging the Status Quo: Teaching with Objects

Early references to the merits of teaching with objects are documented in the work of Moravian philosopher and reformer, John Amos Comenius (1592–1670), considered by many the father of modern education. Comenius recognized the value of learning through *natural experience* with a special emphasis on sensory perception as a means of knowing. His innovative thinking and interest in sensory-based learning challenged traditional schooling methods of memorization and recitation, and introduced a new way of thinking about education. Comenius' innovative thinking defied accepted methods of teaching by recognizing that children learn best when the experience is grounded in objects rather than words. This object-based approach builds on the familiarity of everyday experience which creates a foundation for understanding symbolic language or less well-known objects that are part of formal schooling. His vision led to the idea of aligning text with images or objects to bring abstract concepts to life, thereby enriching the experience of readers through a sense of sight.

Comenius' universally popular textbook, *Orbis Pictus* or *Orbis Sensualium Pictus* [*The Visible World in Pictures*], published in 1658, left an enduring mark on the educational world. The text is widely considered as one of the first picture books for children and uses illustrations to shed light on a wide range of concepts described in the volume. This revolutionary approach sought to strengthen the learning process and increase the emphasis on the concrete object by melding a visual image with the abstract or symbolic representation of written language. Comenius included in his work a multitude of drawings, for example, an image of a cicada to accompany the account of this unique insect; illustrations of different species of birds to complement detailed descriptions; and scenes depicting religious or moral narratives recounted in the textbook. This sensorial approach literally paints a picture for the reader rather than requiring a feat of imagination.

Comenius gained recognition in his lifetime for his groundbreaking text, *Orbis Pictus*, yet his theories of sensorial and object-based learning were largely ignored until the time of Pestalozzi. Theorists who followed Comenius, from Pestalozzi and Froebel to Piaget and Bruner, continued to reflect similar beliefs in formulating their thinking about the process of learning. For example, in 1967, the Swiss philosopher, Jean Piaget quoted Comenius in a discussion of sensation as integral to learning: "the truth and certainty of science depend more on witness of the senses than on anything else" (Piaget [1967] 1993, p. 2). The work of Comenius is recognized as the beginning of "a long educational tradition" valuing sensory experience as essential to learning (Hein 1998, p. 143).

The Object Lesson: A Belief in Natural Education

Nearly 100 years after Comenius, Swiss pedagogue, Johann Pestalozzi (1746–1827) reignited interest in teaching with concrete objects and described his approach with the term "object lessons." Pestalozzi entered the realm of teaching after pursuing a variety of vocations, ultimately becoming a strong advocate for a new form of education. He opened several schools over three decades with a boarding school at Yverdon (1805) being the last and most successful of his efforts. Pestalozzi's progressive pedagogy abandoned traditions of the times and offered a revolutionary model for the education field.

Pestalozzi, much like Comenius, was a proponent of *natural education,* which he defined as a process of learning that nourishes the child through active, sensory-based exploration and "what he termed *Anschauung*: 'object lessons' or direct, concrete observation" (Brosterman 1997, p. 19). His groundbreaking methodologies built on philosophical beliefs arising from influential leaders of the Enlightenment (1685–1815), ideas that emphasized respect for the child and the importance of personal experience as the center of all learning, challenging the status quo of European educational practices and pedagogy. Pestalozzi embraced the notion of child-centered learning and acknowledged the agency of the individual child and the power of *learning by doing,* an attitude that was far from the norm of the day. Pestalozzi believed that the senses serve as the first teacher and that the child, through experience, creates meaning from his interaction with his world.

Pestalozzi grounded his practice in a carefully designed set of principles and techniques to create unique learning environments for students in his progressive schools and those of his protégés. One highly regarded principle states that active learning is a child's most natural state of being and suggests that children build knowledge from the simple to the complex, philosophical beliefs that would later ground the work of another Swiss pedagogue, Jean Piaget.

Objects were valued by Pestalozzi for their sensorial nature and incorporated into all lessons. Stones, shells, nuts, and other commonly found objects were used to teach mathematical concepts as children classified, ordered, and grouped items to develop first-hand knowledge of addition, subtraction, multiplication, and division as well as grapple with other concepts. Object lessons were equally applied to the subjects of geography and science, and often emphasized specimens gathered from nature walks rather than relying on the more typical text or image-driven materials available in schools, such as books and maps (Brosterman 1997).

Pestalozzi's object lessons emphasized active learning, but were also complemented by techniques of observation and drawing. And while drawing held an important place in Pestalozzi's schools, particularly in his experimental approach to teaching the alphabet, the mantra guiding Pestalozzi as an educator and theorist became "things before words, concrete before abstract" (ibid., p. 22).

The Invention of the Kindergarten: Formalization of Objects in the Classroom

Pestalozzi's ideas would be the foundation for Friedrich Froebel's (1782–1852) creation of the kindergarten or the children's garden, a nineteenth-century invention that would have far-reaching implications for the future of education. Froebel studied at the Frankfurt Model School, a program developed by a protégé of Pestalozzi, and later applied the progressive practices of "head, hand, and heart" to his own work in schools, but was also influenced by experiences in his early life.

Friedrich Froebel explored various interests and fields of study prior to his pursuit of education and teaching, but from his earliest days found great inspiration from the German countryside. His career path was unusual, not beginning with a passion for education, but rather an eclectic journey of farming, studies, and military service. His talents and academic interests included "botany, mathematics, architecture, and crystallography" (Tovey 2013, p. 9), all ideas that at their core related to the logic and order of nature. This passion, and way of seeing the world, were intricately woven into the fabric of Froebel's creation of the kindergarten.

Nature was a guiding force throughout Froebel's life. His sincere appreciation of nature and interest in teaching with *real things* led to Froebel's practices of viewing objects as a conduit for awakening the senses to the structure of everything in nature. A spiritual reverence also played an important part in his thinking. While Froebel's love of nature was a reflection of his beloved countryside, his spiritual influence came from his father, a Lutheran minister, and a maternal uncle, also a pastor and Friedrich's guardian from the age of 10 (ibid.). Together, nature and religion were perceived to be in natural harmony and thought to be essential elements of understanding the world. This fundamental belief created the framework for Froebel's kindergarten, a program designed around the flawless structures of nature and focus on active learning.

The invention of the kindergarten was Froebel's most noteworthy accomplishment. The impetus for this specific work addressing the learning of young children arose from his early experience as a classroom teacher working with older children. It was at that point that Froebel realized "that education would never be a force for regenerating society unless there was a provision for the youngest children" (ibid., p. 10). It was this revelation that prompted Froebel's work on educating the young.

In 1837, Froebel opened the first kindergarten in Bad Blankenburg in Prussia, aimed at nurturing the growth of young children. His love and respect for nature with its seemingly perfect form were embedded in his invention of the kindergarten, and similarly in its name, *kinder* representing the human component and *garten*, the natural (Weston 2000). For Froebel, "Kindergarten's universal, perfect, alternative language of geometric form cultivated children's innate ability to observe, reason, express, and create" (Brosterman 1997, p. 12).

In Froebel's pioneering design, there was evidence of Pestalozzi's influence, particularly in the status of objects in the curriculum. Much like Pestalozzi, Froebel viewed objects as exceptional opportunities for learning and used that framework when developing curriculum resources. His carefully crafted materials designed for classroom activity, known as *gifts and occupations,* can easily be construed as the next iteration of object lessons.

Norman Brosterman, author of *Inventing Kindergarten*, artfully describes the centrality of objects in Froebel's approach to schooling and the rationale for employing this technique:

> Froebel made *objective work*, or object teaching, central to his pedagogy, recognizing that the handling of material things aided children in the development of their creative faculties and provided varied and complex experiences through simple means. By examining real things, kindergarten pupils developed originality in thinking and problem solving.
>
> *ibid., p. 34*

Froebel understood the power of objects and through a technique described as *object lessons* encouraged the use of simple, everyday things from nuts and stones to feathers and sticks "to illuminate the processes of growth and unity in nature" (ibid., p. 34). Objects provided for children's play introduced opportunities for creativity, imagination, and problem solving.

Froebel believed that young children "learn best through self-activity, talk, and play" (Tovey 2013, p. 1) and toward that end devised two distinct types of object-centered activities, *gifts and occupations*. These inventions, often considered to be the first educational toys, were essentially resource materials designed to encourage exploration and discovery through open-ended play, intended for kindergartners but also encouraged for use at home with infants and toddlers.

Gifts (numbers 1–9) were thoughtfully conceived sets of objects that had permanent form and were designed to engage children in learning basic concepts of number, form, dimension, and unity. The first *gift*, a set of soft, hand-crocheted balls of various colors (Figure 3.1), was designed to enlighten young children about their world through play and experimentation:

> Perfect in form, the ball, or sphere, was the practical expression of stability and the material expression of motion. By grasping, rolling, dropping, hiding, and swinging the ball, the child gained intuitive and experiential knowledge of object, space, time, color, movement, attraction, union, independence, and gravity.
>
> *Brosterman 1997, p. 42*

Blocks were prominently featured in Froebel's *gifts*. The most basic set of Froebelian blocks is a collection of three objects: a sphere, a cylinder, and a cube, all beautifully crafted from the finest maple or beech trees. Remaining sets of building blocks vary in number and shape, and allow for exploration and discovery, creation of pattern, use of imagination, and discovery. Craftsmanship and aesthetics were very important to Froebel as evident in the beauty of the gifts.

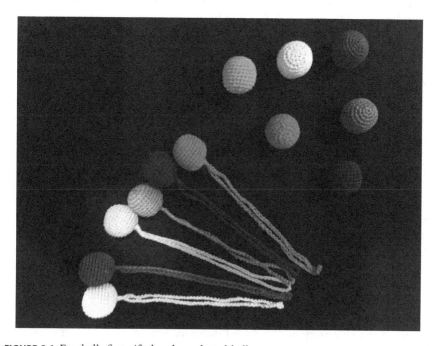

FIGURE 3.1 Froebel's first gift: hand-crocheted balls

Occupations (numbers 10–20) were more plastic, or flexible, and might be categorized as crafts such as cutting, weaving, and paper folding similar to origami and molding of clay. Activities ranged from drawing techniques and stick laying to exploring the concept of lines to peas work for illustrating two and three dimensions as well as volume of objects. Each activity, while using simple objects, sought to introduce both simple and complex ideas related to nature and the manmade environment. Freedom of exploration and creative expression were values inherent in the materials and their use.

Gifts and occupations were considered by Froebel as play objects to pique children's natural curiosity, and according to his writing, to ultimately provide insight into principles of nature. "The twenty gifts and occupations … were designed to harness and direct this natural impulse [curiosity], all the while maintaining the impression that classwork was mostly fun and games" (ibid., p. 13).

Froebel changed the nature of education through his object-centered philosophy of learning for young children. He recognized the value of learning through experiences with the tangible world, primarily through play, but understood the merits of adult facilitation. Essential to Froebel's philosophy was the notion that learning was a product of play and social interaction.

The Development of Progressive Education

The movement toward progressive education has its roots in the work of Comenius and his instinctual belief that tangible objects, particularly those from nature, are essential to a child's learning and should be integrated into schooling, challenging the status quo of his time. In the latter part of the eighteenth century and into the nineteenth century, Pestalozzi and Froebel added to the conversation, advancing pedagogical practices, which "became the foundation of all progressive education to follow" (ibid., p. 20).

Over the next century, progressive education gained support and slowly changed thinking about cognitive development, bringing greater attention to the notion that learning comes from interaction with the environment, thus widening the discussion about objects, and ultimately changed the perception of learning and the path of schools for the future.

John Dewey (1859–1952), widely known for his belief in learning by doing, played a significant role in moving the progressive education agenda forward by bringing attention to experiential learning, an approach that valued personal interaction with the tangible world as essential to constructing meaning. Dewey's pragmatic approach focused on experience in the real world connected to the more mundane events of everyday life, rather than abstractions found in books, with experience broadly defined as interactions with real things as well as social contact.

Dewey profoundly changed the world of schooling with his blend of theory and practice at the University of Chicago's Laboratory School, later referred to as The Dewey School, and in 1899, shared his vision of education with the Chicago community through a series of lectures and later went on to reach a broader audience with the worldwide publication of the lectures. In one lecture, "The School and Society," Dewey explained his rationale for active, experiential learning, a principle vital to his new movement, and brought attention to the differences between traditional education and the progressive school, the former focused primarily on memorization and recitation and the latter centered on children's work or learning by doing:

> The intimate acquaintance got with nature at first hand, with real things and materials, with the actual processes of their manipulation, and the knowledge of their social necessities and uses. In all this there was continual training of observation, of ingenuity, constructive imagination, of logical thought, and of the sense of reality acquired through first-hand contact with actualities.
>
> *Dewey 1900, p. 8*

Dewey was not convinced of the value of "object lessons for the sake of giving information" (ibid., p. 8), but rather believed that it was the social context of the learning by doing that was the best teacher. Authenticity of experience was the ideal for Dewey, from planting a garden for nourishment to shearing sheep, carding wool, and weaving fabric for clothing. For Dewey, the integration of school and society was essential for real learning as a platform for grounded learning in real world phenomena and processes.

One hundred years after the birth of John Dewey, with his work still a source of inspiration, W.F. Warde wrote an article analyzing Dewey's contributions to education reform and included a description of the theorist's understanding of young learners:

> Children soak up knowledge and retain it for use when they are spontaneously induced to look into matters of compelling interest to themselves. They progress fastest in learning, not through being mechanically drilled in prefabricated material, but by doing work, experimenting with things, changing them in purposive ways.
>
> *Warde 1960, p. 9*

The emphasis on experience and active learning endorsed by Dewey, both essential to the progressive movement, became the underpinnings of constructivist learning theory upon which others would build. Swiss psychologist, Jean Piaget took up the mantle and extended notions of constructivism to advance thinking related to this growing set of beliefs. Through extensive observation of children, Piaget developed an understanding of cognitive development and perceived learning to be a process of constructing meaning through interaction with the environment. He believed that the senses are essential to the process and that true understanding occurs when the learner interacts with the physical world through sight, sound, taste, touch, and smell, all possibilities when exploring objects. His beliefs are recognized as aligning with the underlying theories of Comenius, Pestalozzi, and Froebel.

Piaget saw knowledge as a product of past experience integrated with current interactions that are both physical and social. Through human and physical interactions, the senses are the conduit for taking in new information to be analyzed, organized, and interpreted in light of internal, mental constructs formed from previous experience (Piaget 1973).

For Piaget, physical objects contributed significantly to children's learning. He believed that children "must be given opportunities for exploration of materials in order to understand how certain phenomenon take place. It is only through such manipulation of objects that the child can begin to understand the operations of his acts" (Singer and Revenson 1978, p. 109). For example, children learn about physical attributes such as size, shape, color, and texture through their play with a set of blocks. Knowledge comes from manipulation and experimentation. Through trial-and-error, a child discovers that a triangular block is not a sturdy foundation for building a tall structure and that a larger, rectangular block is more effective. In play, the child recognizes similarities and differences in blocks, which leads to forming patterns, sorting, and ordering. Knowledge is gleaned from the physical interaction with objects, an essential element in the process of learning.

In Piaget's world, the ideal is "to present the child with rich problem-solving situations in which the active child learns ... in the course of exploration" (Edwards, Gandini and Forman 2012, p. 57). This principle underlies the work of Piaget and is an essential ingredient in progressive schools, including a program of world renown created in Reggio Emilio, Italy, in the late 1940s by Loris Malaguzzi (1920–1994) and his community (Shaffer 2015, p. 75).

The Reggio Emilia Model: The Object as Inspiration

The Reggio Emilia philosophy incorporated a new appreciation for learning from the natural world with the idea of emergent curriculum stemming from ordinary discoveries and interests of children. The influence of Pestalozzi, Froebel, and Dewey is apparent when examining the philosophical beliefs framing the program. In Reggio-inspired programs, there is respect for children's natural instinct of curiosity to pursue answers to the unknown. Educators recognize children as capable researchers who seek to reveal new information about their world and understand that carefully prepared environments are intended "to awaken in young children powers to perceive, study, and represent the beautiful and orderly worlds of nature and culture surrounding them" (Edwards et al. 2012, p. 368).

The school environment is far more than an empty space or a place to gather, but rather is considered by Reggio educators as an essential component of the learning process, sometimes referred to as the third teacher:

> To act as an educator for the child, the environment has to be flexible: it must undergo frequent modification by the children and the teachers to remain

up-to-date and responsive to their needs to be protagonists in constructing their knowledge. All the things that surround and are used by the people in the school – the objects, the materials, and the structures – are seen not as passive elements but, on the contrary, as elements that condition and are conditioned by the actions of children and adults who are active in it.

ibid., p. 339

Objects selected by teachers play a distinctive role in Reggio programs. Everyday objects or specimens from nature are introduced into the environment to inspire children to think, question, and pursue knowledge, an approach often described as a *provocation*. In this sense, the term *provocation* is defined as an opportunity to provoke thinking, spark interest, initiate discussion, encourage creativity, and arouse curiosity about the object or a collection of objects as a strategy to engage children in making meaning about their world. For example, seeds collected from trees or gardens and arranged on a classroom table serve as a provocation to encourage observation, inspire reflection, and ignite conversation. In Reggio classrooms, children look closely, make observations, analyze and compare specimens, ask questions aroused by their exploration, seek expert advice from a variety of sources, and draw conclusions based upon their experience. The provocation, in this case, seeds and seedpods, is the catalyst that leads to exploration and, ultimately, construction of knowledge.

The idea that children learn through close encounters with their environment extends beyond personal interaction with objects to the creative expression of ideas through the use of a wide range of materials. In fact, a specially-designed art studio, the *atelier*, serves as a laboratory where children experiment with materials – paper, fabric, clay, stones, shells, seeds, and more – and express ideas that arise from multi-disciplinary, classroom projects. In this process, children come to understand different points of view as they delve deeply into complex problems. The atelier is a place of research, exploration, discovery, and expression.

Insiders from Reggio Emilia speak of a "theory of the hundred languages of children – the many ways that children express themselves, tell stories, and experiment" (Edwards et al. 2012, p. 176). Art-making in the atelier supports children in expressing their ideas. This theory honors children's natural inclinations toward learning to encompass the multiple perspectives that children bring to meaning-making and the pathways taken to create that meaning. The limitless ways that children interact with and interpret their world reflect one of the highest values of the Reggio Emilia philosophy.

Progressive Education and Museums

The idea of learning through experience so highly valued by Reggio-inspired educators, as well as their many progressive counterparts past and present, continued to gain prominence in the work of educational theorists and practitioners throughout the twentieth century. According to noted educational historian,

Lawrence Cremin, "progressive education ultimately became common coin in America, and perhaps elsewhere in the world as well" (Gardner 1991, p. 194). Ideas arising from within the constructivist framework advanced by the progressive movement, including project-based learning, afforded students, particularly those in elementary and early childhood classrooms, more authentic experiences through interactions with the real thing or objects that make up the world.

It is important to note that the practice of teaching with objects, and later the progressive movement, is more closely connected to school-based environments, particularly in the days of Comenius, Pestalozzi, and Froebel, but crossed boundaries into other educational realms more than one hundred years ago to include informal learning environments, such as museums. This was particularly true of the theories and practices of John Dewey, which were heralded by individuals working in museums as well as schools.

As research on cognitive development continued in the latter half of the twentieth century, the principles of progressive education remained of interest to leaders in the field. One leader, Harvard professor and developmental psychologist, Howard Gardner (1943–), introduced his theory of multiple intelligences, suggesting that human beings possess many different ways of knowing and expressing ideas. His views challenged traditional beliefs about intelligence and acknowledged the relationship of experience to learning. In his texts, Gardner recognizes the values and practices of progressive education as promising and extends the conversation about learning to settings beyond the classroom and into museum galleries. It is in the context of museums where Gardner touches upon the idea of authenticity, referring to the perception of originality and suggests the idea of something that is real rather than an imitation of the original. With the ability to reproduce almost any object with little effort, society developed an affinity for the original and cast aside the imitation. In some cases, individuals would argue that a replica is equal to the original artifact or specimen, but the social construct valuing authenticity gives the original greater weight. Similar to other progressivists, Gardner places a high value on the object.

This starting point in a conversation about authenticity is developmentally appropriate for the young child, even though there are myriad interpretations of *authenticity*, many of which are more complex and sophisticated when compared to the simplistic thinking that grounds a child's initial understanding of the term. Greater exploration of the term makes sense as cognitive abilities mature.

Learning from authentic objects, many displayed with visual context that may be lacking in a typical classroom, is widely recognized as an advantage that comes from museum experiences. An informal setting, such as a museum, contrasts with the more typical school setting where concepts are explored in the vacuum of a classroom often without appropriate, meaningful context of the real world.

The museum offers a broad range of opportunities for learning and allows for the different intellectual strengths and aptitudes of children. Exhibitions in children's museums, and more and more so in traditional museums of the twenty-first century, tap into the sensorimotor capacities of young learners. These environments encourage interaction with experts as well as engagement with artifacts and specimens. The broad and diverse resources of many museums provide increased opportunities for developing what Gardner terms *genuine understanding* and which he describes as "a still-alluring educational vision" (Gardner 1991, p. 199).

Gardner's theories bridge the world of formal and informal learning, providing shared goals and a common language for discourse on teaching with objects and the place of museums in educating society's children. Museums' historical commitment to education through objects – artifacts, natural specimens, and works of art – acquired new meaning for the institution of schooling with the development of progressive education.

Teaching and Learning from Objects

As the history of progressive education suggests, experience is essential to learning and interaction with the physical environment is one aspect of the learning process. The ability to use one's senses – sight, sound, taste, touch, and smell – through physical interaction with an object, introduces information and provides an opportunity for insight that contributes to constructing meaning about the object, and thus, about the world. This natural approach to learning, driven by curiosity or a desire to know, is not exclusive to specific settings, but rather crosses the boundaries of informal and formal environments.

The museum, with a mission to collect, study, preserve, and interpret objects, offers a range of opportunities for learning through objects. This is, in fact, a topic of discourse within the museum field today and one that can be traced to the social progressive era of the early twentieth century and subsequently to the years following World War II as museum education "matured into an acknowledged profession" (Hein 2011, p. 340). Educational theories of the progressive era crossed boundaries between formal learning environments of schooling and informal settings of museums.

In the children's museum movement, objects were initially exhibited in a fashion similar to traditional museums where visitors explore objects visually. This practice changed significantly when Anna Billings Gallup arrived at the Brooklyn Children's Museum in 1902. In her role as curatorial assistant, Gallup introduced a sensory-based, interactive approach to learning that remains a hallmark defining children's museums today.

During the social progressive movement, the practice of teaching with objects in museums held great appeal for a select group of museum professionals. One noted advocate, John Cotton Dana (1856–1929), advanced the idea of teaching with objects in his work as librarian and museum director, using the collections of the Newark Museum to enrich the lives of everyday citizens in the community. He envisioned his work as an experiment in museum practices with great emphasis on serving the public and focused attention on educational work by encouraging museums to share their collections and "to lend to teachers objects, just as the library lends books and pictures" (Peniston 1999, p. 163) to support education. In a

1921 report documenting the experimental practices at the Newark Museum, John Cotton Dana highlighted object-based opportunities for children:

> For several months, as long in fact as space therefore could be found in quarters which each month were more crowded, the museum gave up a room to a group of objects and pictures selected, installed, and labeled with special references to the interests of young people. It was, in effect, a children's museum.
>
> *ibid., p. 163*

The practice of teaching with objects is embraced by most educators working in museums and acknowledged as an effective teaching strategy for those working with younger children. Even as educational theorists recognize the value of object-based experience in learning, the practice is not universally accepted by the formal education field.

Conclusion

There is a well-documented history of teaching with objects. From the groundbreaking work of Comenius to the creation of Froebel's kindergarten and its carefully designed object lessons, respect for the object as an integral element of learning has garnered widespread interest and brought educators together from formal and informal settings.

The notion of teaching with objects was introduced in the context of formal schooling, but later moved beyond the classroom to gain widespread acceptance in museums throughout the twentieth century. As museum educators expanded their role in working with the public, particularly children, their efforts focused on developing programs that would more fully engage visitors in making meaning about objects and collections. The *object lesson*, an approach that inspires learning through interaction with the real thing, is part of the history of schooling and museums, yet still important in today's conversation about learning.

4

OBJECT-BASED LEARNING: MAKING MEANING FROM OBJECTS

> Child and man alike are somewhat moved to interest, appreciation, clear understanding, and development of their powers by reading of a thing or process; they are still more moved by seeing the actual thing or process and learning of it through the ear; still more by handling and hearing and asking questions and receiving replies; and most of all by trying, under skilled guidance, to produce the thing or to repeat the process.
>
> *John Cotton Dana, in Peniston (1999), p. 89*

Introduction

Museum professionals recognize the power of objects and understand them to be a source of information and insight. Without artifacts and scientific specimens, historians and scientists representing a wide range of subjects would be limited in their research and study. Just as the object serves a vital role in the work of professional researchers, the object introduces a wide range of opportunities for the everyday learner. As noted by John Cotton Dana, an intimate association with an object or process reaches a level of understanding that surpasses anything that can come from other sources of information.

And while there are many techniques for teaching with objects, one of the most common strategies is in-depth exploration, an approach focused on understanding various perspectives. To reveal the many layers of information, a process of careful examination is essential and requires an open mind. A second strategy is less about the object itself, but more about the relationship of the object to another object or context. This strategy defines the object as an entry point to gain insight or greater understanding of a related object. A third strategy uses the object as a provocation, to provoke or inspire the viewer. Each strategy is discussed as a broad approach that is relevant for all learners, but also includes references for children's learning. These suggestions offer a starting point for thinking about the many possibilities for teaching with objects, but are simply a few of the potential opportunities that museum educators and classroom teachers can consider.

In-Depth Exploration of Objects

Objects help us to imagine and understand moments from the past by providing historical context and insight into the people, events, and values of the time; they are a lens through which we view traditions and beliefs about diverse cultures and forge meaning about others and their ways; they are a window into the natural world and provide the ability to understand its functions. And while it is possible to identify attributes or a set of truths about a given object – in the case of a manmade object, the date or place of origin, the history of ownership, or physical attributes such as material, size, shape, and style – there are some characteristics or values that are defined by the individual and not necessarily the same for everyone. Beauty, for example, is understood in different ways and specific to each human being. Personal exploration reveals information and allows for individual interpretation.

As a strategy, in-depth exploration seeks to engage the learner actively in a process of gathering information through the senses of sight, sound, taste, touch, and smell. This approach is particularly salient for the young child as a sensory learner. Information gleaned from interaction with an object can be documented in many ways, aligning strategies with developmental levels of visitors. Older students can express ideas through written narrative or poetry, discreetly describing observations and assumptions, while the pre-literate child can share ideas through drawing, photo documentation, and role play or dictate personal thoughts and interpretative ideas to a companion.

Younger, less-experienced children will be able to take part in analysis of their findings with appropriate guidance shaped by thoughtful questions. For more sophisticated learners, the process is more complex. Data, collected in the process of careful looking and attention to detail as well as from thoughtful questioning and analysis, leads to hypotheses or logical conclusions, and serves as a starting point for further research, a necessary step to compare findings and test ideas in the context of what is known. What becomes clear in any process of in-depth exploration is that some information may never surface while other details are easily retrieved or identified simply by close looking. The goal is to explore, imagine, and pique curiosity.

The idea of learning through careful looking is the subject of a wide range of research-based articles and books in the museum field. One research-based approach represented in the literature, "Making Thinking Visible," is a program developed by experts at Harvard's Project Zero. The approach emphasizes careful looking as a means of examining and understanding the process of thinking. Structured experiences described as *Thinking Routines* offer a series of focused questions to guide looking and responding, yet there is also fluidity in the process. The framework or routine serves as scaffolding for the learning process and creates a culture of thinking that is applicable to other experiences. Careful looking is an important first step in Project Zero's model.

Museum educators are typically well-versed in the concept of looking and cite a 1990 publication, *Learning from Objects* (Durbin, Morris, and Wilkinson, 1990), as an excellent source of information. The publication offers a detailed text that shares a favored method of investigating objects which is best described as a process of questioning related to physical features, construction, function, design, and value of an object. This approach encourages careful looking to gather evidence, connect to prior knowledge, and critically analyze the data to make meaning and understand context. The authors recognize the value of observation as a tool for constructing knowledge and believe that discoveries emerge as part of personal interaction with objects. Young investigators learn that the design or construction of an artifact offers hints about purpose or function; evidence or wear such as dents, chips, uneven edges, or faded color can indicate an object's age when considered in the context of its design; special marks or symbols may indicate the place or time of an object's creation. Even young children recognize that an object might be considered old, as opposed to new, based on its physical features that indicate wear.

Learning from Objects presents a robust argument for hands-on exploration of objects. The strategy clearly rests with sensory-based exploration as a means of collecting information, but acknowledges the critical nature of further research and discussion to test ideas or draw conclusions.

This model of learning from objects is multi-faceted, existing on a continuum with thoughtful study that ranges from the very simple to the exceedingly complex. A novice exploring objects for the first time is likely to approach the experience in a simplistic fashion, with information gathered primarily through the sense of sight; over time, exploration of objects becomes more sophisticated as individuals gain experience, and thereby, refine skills, increase focus on different senses for gathering data, and acknowledge the multi-layered meanings of objects. The locus of learning is defined by the interaction with the object.

The idea of object-based learning is widely understood and highly valued within the museum field, yet variations are found in the terminology used or sequence of actions describing how to learn from objects. Some approaches are specific to engaging museum visitors, while others represent the role of the museum professional as researcher.

Montpelier, the home of James Madison, offers its visitors a way to think about its artifacts through an exhibition, "The Presidential Detective Story," which details the steps used by museum experts to accurately identify objects relevant to the life of this president. At the core of this process is the concept of authenticity, a time-honored characteristic of museums, and thus, an essential element for this museum in analyzing artifacts chosen to portray the life and times of Madison. The four-step process commences with a careful examination of each artifact to consider style, size, material, maker's mark, and construction, a starting point for the historical research. Information gleaned through sensory exploration is also analyzed in the context of what is already known about the person and time period, in this case, James Madison and his presidency. A broad net is cast in search of primary sources, such as diaries, letters, or wills to expand the base of facts for interpretation. Further data is gathered through scientific methodologies as well as technology with processes such as paint analysis, fabric examination, archaeological excavation, or architectural investigation. Scientific findings pinpoint time periods or geographic locations specific to origins of objects. The final stage of investigation is defined as tracking the clues from earlier steps using the expertise of researchers, searching a multitude of databases, and reviewing thousands of objects that represent relevant collections. Although this particular process reflects the work of museum experts, this concept of mining objects to acquire knowledge is not dissimilar to the process advocated for the novice. The difference is in the scope and complexity of the study.

The young child will capably make observations about an object, particularly in regard to its physical features, and will also ask relevant questions that demonstrate a focus on detail. One child's observation becomes a source of conversation for peers as children express opinions about an object. For example, a dinosaur skeleton at a natural history museum prompts a discussion about the characteristics of the prehistoric animal and its habits. The children accurately note the size of the dinosaur and its general shape, but disagree about its eating preferences. One child notices the pointed teeth and suggests that this creature was a carnivore or meat eater. The children compare the teeth of several dinosaurs, some being flat while others are sharp, and decide that this information is a clue that they will explore. Observations, questions, and interpretations are part of a larger discussion facilitated by a more knowledgeable adult.

Experienced museum educators encounter a wide variety of object-based methodologies in professional articles and texts, and recognize similarities inherent in each. Interpretation of objects relies heavily on sensory interaction with an artifact, specimen, or work of art as a foundation for analysis and suggests further research leading to greater understanding and clarity.

The strategy of in-depth exploration becomes clear with an example of a simple artifact. At first glance, the object portrayed in Figure 4.1 is seemingly unfamiliar, at least to most people, but through observation and sensory exploration it is possible to lay the groundwork for understanding the artifact and to make meaning about its place in society. The process of in-depth exploration begins with the obvious, looking at the physical attributes or features, a step essential to constructing meaning by using the attributes as building blocks for comparing, questioning, and analyzing. (Note: Readers can examine the image in Figure 4.1 to create a list of statements about the artifact based on the evidence, but of course, interaction with the real thing is far more effective. Much is missed when sensory interaction is limited.) The simple exercise described below offers some insight into the approach that includes a more sensory-based experience.

The evidence gathered from observation and interaction with this artifact tells us that:

Object-Based Learning   49

FIGURE 4.1 Primitive soap saver

- The object is approximately 10 inches in length and light in weight, only a few ounces.
- This object is made of wood and metal, possibly several different metals.
- The colors of the object are natural to the materials, silver, gray, and brassy gold for the metals and shades of brown for the wood.
- The object is made up of several parts that are fitted together to act as one piece, with one part long and narrow, possibly functioning as a handle, and the other part a rectangular wire basket that can be opened and closed and used to hold some unknown material.
- The object appears to be old and somewhat worn.
- There is a distinct smell or scent around the wire basket, an unexpected freshness.
- It is not clear as to whether the object was mass-produced or handmade; some parts are not carefully constructed (the wire basket) while other parts (the handle) seem to have uniformity in the construction.

Once observations are documented, the study continues with an analysis from the comparison of the unfamiliar object with other more familiar items with similar features. *What is it about the design or construction of this object that is like other more familiar objects? What is suggested by the design?* The design of our unknown object begs the question of what is kept in the wire basket. In a group setting, curious minds interested in the purpose of the artifact take part in a robust brainstorming session where ideas are wide-ranging and include diverse opinions from a tea diffuser to a tool for cooking chestnuts or other edibles over an open fire. This discussion is likely to reflect older, more sophisticated visitors. Younger children often base their responses on an object's physical features and then generate a list of possibilities of what the object might be with ideas ranging from a magic wand to an unusual shovel or scoop. Although a preschooler's ideas may seem irrelevant to the average adult, their associations are typically based on personal experience and are often quite literal in nature. It is helpful to ask children to explain their ideas with a simple phrase: *Tell me why you think that.* It is often surprising the connections that children make.

Regardless of age, the soapy fragrance is a clue indicating that the object is a tool for cleaning or washing. A few simple questions frame the conversation for younger children and encourage them to think critically about the meaning of the scent. *What do you notice when you smell the object? Is it like any other smells that you know? What do you think this tells us about the object?* Careful analysis and discussion bring the suggestions in line with the facts and eliminate those where logic suggests implausibility. Some comparisons lead to a series of hypotheses requiring further study and research that confirm or refute the proposed ideas.

A quick search of the Web using the clues obtained from observation combined with prior knowledge leads to a Depression era image that mirrors our unknown artifact in almost every detail. The accompanying description sheds light on previous thoughts and conclusions.

> 1930's Depression Era Soap Saver was used to make sure no amount of soap was wasted in a time when most could not afford to be wasteful. You would have kept your soap and soap bits in this and swished it around in the sink, wash tub, or bath then it would have been hung up so soap could dry.
>
> *Texoma Vintage, www.etsy.com*

The pooled information offers deeper understanding. Interestingly, knowledge of the artifact would be broadened by turning to an elderly neighbor or relative who experienced the Depression first-hand. This object unknown to the younger generations of today would likely be familiar to most Americans living in the 1930s. Oral history surrounding this artifact would enrich and contribute significantly to the learning process. The artifact would take on greater meaning if our resident expert from the 1930s were to demonstrate the use of the object, mentoring others in the group. In this way, in-depth exploration that involves activity follows the lead of John Cotton Dana, one of museum's strongest advocates for object-based learning.

Some objects such as the soap saver may be more relevant for children aged 10 and older as they begin to study the past, but with the right approach, it is possible to find a connection for younger children as well. Just focus on the broad notion that it's important not to be wasteful and connect the concept to something in a young child's life, reminding children that many things are precious and not to be wasted. Complete the conversation with an explanation that this object was used a long time ago to save tiny pieces of soap so that they were not wasted.

For young children visiting museums, it is important to select an object that has a sense of novelty, yet can have relevance for them and connect to something that they know. For example, the Bata Shoe Museum in Toronto, Canada, houses a wide array of unusual footwear, including padukas, worn by holy men and others in India. With a simple sole and a wooden knob or post, the shoe is not easily recognizable yet with a little guidance and open-ended questioning, children quickly see the similarity between this unfamiliar object and more familiar sandals. While initially unfamiliar, there are connections that children can make to their everyday lives. The hands-on aspect of this experience could be handling a more typical sandal or flip-flop and comparing this object to the museum object. Guided research following the gallery experience gives children additional information.

Selecting the right object for in-depth exploration is more likely to engage young children in the process of learning through objects. The process of discovery that comes from this open-ended inquiry and research is exhilarating and builds a variety of skills for children across developmental domains of language, logic, and social interaction while also acquainting children with people and places from around the world and across time.

The Object as Entry Point

Objects, powerful in their own right, offer opportunities to engage children in thinking about a variety of ideas or concepts. It is the relationship between the initial object and other artifacts, natural specimens, or works of art that is essential to this strategy. A simple object, when carefully selected, sheds light on something less well known, yet has value beyond that to allow for greater understanding through sensory experience. A collection of fabric samples – lace, velvet, silk, burlap, tulle – can change the way that children look at and interpret portraits or other paintings. Although sophisticated painters capture the look of a lace collar or velveteen waistcoat, a child's experience with these materials is likely limited. The chance to touch the real thing, or in this case similar materials of varied textures, redefines the looking and opens an opportunity for discussion about different types of fabric as well as the idea of wealth and socio-economic levels. As children examine a piece of lace, they are able to see the detail and craftsmanship, and are able to compare the actual material with the painter's interpretation. The texture of more luxurious fabrics like velvet and satin appears in stark contrast with burlap or cotton, even in the eyes of a child. *Which of these materials would feel good next to your skin? Would most people like the soft, smooth material or the rough material as clothing? What makes you think that?* In this context, children are introduced to the idea that some materials cost more money than others and that few families can afford clothing made from these expensive materials. There is a direct connection made between the better fabric and the wealth of the person in the portrait. The tactile experience enhances understanding and changes the lens through which portraits or paintings are viewed. Although the concept is complex, it is introduced on a simplistic level. This strategy is incorporated into many children's programs in art museums where educators recognize the value of sensory experience.

An object also serves as an entry point by infusing a perspective beyond the tactile connection, even though it is often through touch that new ideas are conveyed. For example, children are often surprised to find that the toe of a ballerina's shoe is a hard, flat surface, unlike their own shoe, and yet they quickly integrate this newly found information into their discussion of paintings of ballet such as *Two Dancers on a Stage* by Edgar Degas in the Courtauld Gallery, London. Preschoolers enthusiastically make the connection between the construction of the toe shoe and the ballerina's ability to dance on her toes. A mere description of the toe shoe's hardness is far less meaningful for any child compared to the hands-on experience with the actual object.

At times, an object seems so simple that educators miss an opportunity to create a memorable experience for young visitors. An empty Mason jar appears mundane at best and hardly worthy of a gallery experience, but it's amazing how this unassuming object can capture the attention of children and focus their thinking during a conversation about Victory Gardens or serve as an introduction to other historical exhibitions related to the Depression Era. Simple questions open the conversation and allow children to add their voice and ideas to the experience. *What is this object? Where would you find an object like this? How might it be useful?* The conversation invites personal interaction and at the same time serves as an entry point into broader concepts developed in the exhibition. The Mason jar symbolizes frugality at a particular time in our history when canning fruits and vegetables from family gardens was necessary, and encourages children to look at other objects and environments portrayed in museums from this era. History museums across the country are filled with exhibitions representing life in the early twentieth century where a Mason jar would be an appropriate introduction. "Within These Walls," an exhibition at the Smithsonian Institution's National Museum of American History, displays World War II era artifacts such as cookbooks and rationing coupons, a story that is easily expanded to the idea of Victory Gardens. A simple Mason jar, while not necessarily on view, is a meaningful entry point as a tangible object that introduces ideas embedded in the exhibition.

Objects provide an opportunity to build a bridge between the child and artifacts on display in exhibitions or with works of art. Children often encounter the unknown when looking at exhibitions representing historical or cultural stories beyond the child's neighborhood, but a simple, familiar object provides a tangible connection between the child and the museum content. At the Palace Museum in Beijing, China, also known as the Forbidden City, there are exquisite ancient bells on display that look nothing like bells of today. By making a connection to a small, traditionally-shaped bell, children easily recognize the relationship to artifacts in the gallery. The bell is a perfect entry point for making the connection to the artifacts in the exhibition. This strategy is equally effective in the preschool classroom when introducing an unfamiliar object or idea.

The object as entry point is a strategy that works with young children as well as more experienced museum visitors, in classrooms and galleries, and is effective in cultivating interest and interpretative experiences related to art, science, history, and culture. It adds a tactile experience to the visual, serving as a catalyst for thinking broadly about objects and their relationships. And whether it is an everyday object like a seedpod or a more majestic specimen like a sparkling geode, interesting and meaningful connections can be made between an object and a broader topic represented in text, art, or collections. The object as entry point is a powerful interpretative tool.

An Object as Provocation

Provocation is a word with many meanings. The most appropriate for defining this particular strategy is "something that provokes, arouses, or stimulates" (*Merriam-Webster Dictionary* 2016). It is a term at times associated with negative connotations, but in this instance, the intention is positive and seeks to encourage or expand a child's thinking through the use of an object or event.

This idea of a provocation is prominent today in the early childhood field, particularly in programs inspired by the Reggio Emilia philosophy. In the school setting, provocations are typically objects displayed in classrooms or found in outdoor spaces to encourage exploration of a specific concept that is part of a class study. Interpretations of the term *provocation* vary from school to school and country to country, but a common thread is the goal of encouraging thinking and the expression of ideas.

A provocation can be an everyday object ranging from a teapot to a pinecone or it can be a rare or treasured museum artifact, specimen, or work of art. Whatever the object, the idea is to inspire and elicit a desire to know more, with the object serving as a catalyst. Beyond the idea of knowing is a desire to imagine what might have been or could be. A child looks at an ancient throne and wonders about the king who sat in this majestic chair. *What would it feel like to be a king? How would I spend my day?* Create a pretend throne using a small box or chair and invite children one by one to become the king sitting on the throne. *How would you sit? What would you be wearing? What else would be in the throne room?* Tapping into imagination aligns with the learning style of young children as they seek to understand their world. It is an intuitive approach to learning that opens the door to playful encounters, another natural inclination for children. Play is the bedrock of development for children and serves as an opportunity for exploration and discovery. It builds on a child's curiosity and a desire to know.

In the life of a child, imagination engenders play. This makes sense when thinking about the definition of imagination, "the act or power of forming a mental image of something not present to the senses" (ibid.). The mental image formed in response to the provocation drives physical activity stemming from a child's need to re-enact her thoughts. A child sees a birchbark canoe (the provocation) and imagines paddling down a river surrounded by enormous trees. The idea naturally leads to movement that echoes paddling a canoe through the water.

Play allows a child to interpret and reinterpret perceptions of the world based on experience, and thus, acquire "important developmental, social, and cognitive skills, as well as positive inner traits, that help form the basis for happiness, productivity, and a healthy future" (Perry, Hogan, and Marlin 2000, p.11). Play and imagination go hand-in-hand.

Museums are rich environments for sparking a child's imagination and inspiring play. This is as true for art museums or botanic gardens as it is for museums of history and culture. A few examples will demonstrate how objects serve as an inspiration or catalyst for imagining. A visit to the National Museum of the American Indian (Smithsonian Institution, Washington, DC) is rich in cultural artifacts, many with great appeal for young children. The Osage Cradleboard (1890) is a unique artifact that has the power to provoke thinking. The idea of a mother carrying her baby on her back, secured to a flat board, intrigues children. The beauty of this Native American baby carrier with its intricate patterns, beads, and bells suggests a deep love for the child and a caring mother. Almost any child will eagerly step into the role of mother and take part in pretend play that includes the use of a cradleboard. Some children will want to become the baby swaddled in cloth and imagine the feelings that might engender. The object becomes a provocation for storytelling as children imagine a tale that includes the artifact.

Another example comes from the Bata Shoe Museum, a museum that offers a wide range of diverse footwear, each pair with a specific story (Figure 4.2). The possibilities for provocation are endless. One idea is connected to Mojaris, beautifully appointed saffron shoes worn by temple dancers. The shoes, finely embroidered with intricate designs, are decorated with jade beads and tiny brass bells that jingle when the dancer moves. *What would it feel like to wear these shoes? Can you*

FIGURE 4.2 Mojaris, Hyderabad, c. 1790–1820
Source: Collection of the Bata Shoe Museum. Image copyright ©2017 Bata Shoe Museum, Toronto.

imagine the dancer's clothing? How would the dancer move and what sounds would you hear? The shoes serve as a provocation to inspire thinking and ultimately engage the children in connecting with the artifacts. A natural response to these questions inspires movement and imaginative play. Ideally, the choice of shoes would relate to an area of classroom study or specific interest of the children. Perhaps the class is studying dance and learning about the many different types of dance around the world. Looking at photographs of dancers and costumes prior to the museum visit creates context for the children's gallery experience and enhances learning, but seeing the real thing introduces a level of understanding that is more personal and meaningful.

The idea of using an object to inspire might have less to do with historic context or cultural experience and more to do with freely imaging an unknown. A painting such as Degas' *At the Old Opera House* in the National Gallery of Art, Washington, DC, serves as a provocation for children to imagine what it might be like to perform in a beautiful opera house. *As the dancer, what would you wear? How would you prepare for the performance? Who else would be in the theater? What would happen at the end of the performance?* To go beyond conversation and engage children in play, provide costumes and music appropriate for a classical ballet and show an excerpt from a classical ballet to spur children's imagination about being on stage. Invite children to perform for their peers, wearing headpieces, scarves, or other simple props. Remember to talk about the role of the audience and have simple flowers cut from paper to present at the curtain call as the performance ends. In many ways, this interpretative play is about imagining the before and after as well as the nuances and details of the scene and the accompanying emotions. This is art interpretation!

At times, the provocation is unrelated to other objects and simply serves as a starting point for imaginative thinking. A ballet slipper or more specifically a toe shoe as provocation encourages storytelling about the dancer. *Imagine for a moment. How do you feel when wearing this shoe? What music do you hear when you're dancing?* Children imagine the story and create their own narrative.

An interesting object has great potential for inspiring imagination. Think about Joan Miro's sculpture of Lunar Bird at the Hirshhorn Museum and Sculpture Garden, Smithsonian Institution, Washington, DC, a bird unlike any other bird. When children look closely at Lunar Bird, it is a starting point for creative imagining about birds, real or fanciful. *What makes a bird a bird? If you could create a new species of bird, what would it look like? What makes your bird unique, different from all others?* Miro's sculpture serves as a catalyst for creative thinking and certainly encourages playfulness. It also encourages children to fashion their own images of birds, perhaps in clay sculptures or creative collage.

Provocations add a dimension to learning by introducing an element not previously considered. Objects from the everyday world – a collection of seeds from the outdoor environment, an interesting photograph, or a carpenter's ruler – are plentiful and offer a multitude of opportunities to spark children's curiosity and increase engagement.

Conclusion

Museums have great respect for objects, now and in the past, and exhibit artifacts and specimens to educate and provide pleasure to the public. And while the understanding and interpretation of objects have changed in the past three decades, they continue to be vital to the mission and role that museums play in communities. Just as beliefs about objects have evolved, so will strategies for engaging audiences in connecting with the treasures of the world.

Museum educators in the twenty-first century are engaging young children more and more with objects due to the increased interest in museums exhibited by parents, public officials, and media. Understanding the vast array of object-based strategies, those represented by the work of colleagues as well as those gleaned through other sources such as this text, strengthens and enriches the programming developed by museum educators.

5

LEARNING TO LOOK AT OBJECTS: A PROCESS OF DISCOVERY

> I know of nothing more inspiring than that of making discoveries for oneself.
>
> *George Washington Carver*

Looking Closely, Making Discoveries

Discovery as an educational practice is highly valued in many learning circles, particularly within the early childhood field. It places the learner in an active role and encourages meaning making which fits naturally with what is known about how children learn. Discovery requires time for exploration and the opportunity for close examination of objects for the purpose of gaining new information, or in some cases, confirming what is already known. For most educators, the active child-centered nature of discovery defines its value as an educational tool.

Active learning, where children have the opportunity to explore, aligns with constructivist theory with its focus on child-centered participation, particularly if the process is open-ended. Within the framework of constructivist theory, knowledge is created internally and defined as unique to each individual; in this manner, knowledge gleaned from the discovery process reflects the individual's understanding of the experience rather than simply conforming to external expectations without thought or understanding.

Discovery, described by George Hein (1998) "as a particular type of educational theory" (p. 25), emphasizes the role of the learner as interacting with the physical environment, actively engaged "in the process, whether it is building something, solving a puzzle, handling objects, or otherwise engaging with the 'stuff' of the world" (ibid., p. 31). It is this process that allows the individual to realize or access knowledge that exists in the external world through opportunities to explore, reflect on discoveries, refine ideas, and gain input from a range of sources. The belief is that the learner will discover truth through her interactions with the world and construct meaning from personal experience. Hein notes that "the term 'discovery learning' … has been used as a synonym for any form of education that attributes active participation to the learner" (ibid., p. 31).

Discovery learning is rooted in the child-centered beliefs of the Enlightenment and then more fully articulated in the theories of John Dewey (1859–1952), Lev Vygotsky (1896–1934), and Jean Piaget (1896–1980). It is a model of learning advanced in the 1960s through the work of Jerome Bruner and continues to be important in educational circles today. In Bruner's *Toward a Theory of Instruction*, he suggests that, through discovery, children gain competence and a sense of "confidence in their ability to operate independently" (Bruner 1966, p. 96). He further describes *internal discovery* as reflection that leads to associations with prior knowledge and considers this to be of utmost value, a concept central to constructivist theory. Bruner's work is known for honoring children as learners and believing that they deserve "respect for their own powers of thinking, for their power to generate good questions, to come up with interesting informed guesses" (ibid., p. 96). His writings offer educators justification for the practice of discovery-oriented experiences in museums and classrooms.

As an instructional design model, discovery learning encourages in-depth exploration and increased engagement. These features are recognized as essential skills in scientific thinking and touted by experts in the science community. Dr. Ruth Wilson, author of "Promoting the Development of Scientific Thinking," suggests that "young children are naturally curious and passionate about learning" and "prone to poking, pulling, tasting, pounding, shaking and experimenting" in pursuit of knowledge (2002, p. 1), actions that evolve naturally in a child's attempt to explore and discover. Wilson believes that for the young learner, science is not about content, but rather about the behaviors associated with investigation or problem-solving and refers to these behaviors as "sciencing," indicative of active learning.

Eleanor Duckworth, a Piagetian scholar, also emphasizes the process of learning over content and understands that questions are quintessential elements of learning, with teachers posing open-ended questions that inspire students to think and supporting student-inspired queries. Like Wilson, Duckworth (2006) stresses active engagement as key to learning and insists that science and other ways of knowing are best described as "the having of wonderful ideas" and the ability to act on those ideas (p. 1). She suggests that children learn more through self-discovery, even when conclusions are initially incorrect, than from someone providing direct instruction, and indicates that wonderful ideas are more likely to develop in content areas where there is interest and familiarity. For example, 4-year-old Josie takes an interest in backyard birds and asks questions about their nesting and eating habits. The local hardware store's supply of birdhouses and feeders renews her interest and leads to a wonderful idea. Josie wants to know if all birdhouses or feeders are the same or if some structures will be more appealing or appropriate than others. She clearly wants to know which birdhouse or feeder is best for her backyard birds. Over several days, the family acquires three birdhouses, one that

Josie creates with a little assistance from her mother, a second birdhouse purchased at the hardware store, and a third birdfeeder discovered in the family's garage. Josie watches eagerly as these newly acquired birdhouses and feeders are mounted in the backyard. Over the next few weeks, observation and documentation become an important element of Josie's morning routine and help her construct theories about birds and their habits. A wonderful idea is born out of Josie's interest and curiosity! According to Duckworth, "wonderful ideas do not spring out of nothing" (ibid., p. 6), but rather build on other wonderful ideas. The aim is to explore and uncover what is unknown and be inventive in pursuit of intellectual problems that are real to a child.

Discovery Learning in Museums

Discovery as a method of learning is well documented in museums, from educational programs of the early twentieth century associated with school journeys or fieldtrips to the museum to programs of present day. In the 1960s, the idea of discovery or exploratory learning grew as an educational strategy, building on the theories of Harvard scholar, Jerome Bruner (1915–2016) and ultimately emerging in a few select museums. On America's West Coast, discovery learning developed under the leadership of Frank Oppenheimer at the Exploratorium in San Francisco with his innovative approach privileging exploration and discovery in galleries. At the same time, museum director Michael Spock and his team of professionals at the Boston Children's Museum were experimenting with new ideas that turned attention to discovery learning and "the joys of touching" (Madden and Paisley-Jones 1987, p. 2). By the late 1960s and into the 1970s, the work of Oppenheimer and Spock had brought about a new wave of interest in active learning and more participatory experience in museums, and thus, the formation of discovery spaces less familiar to previous generations visiting traditional museums. With the opening of discovery zones and hands-on discovery carts, sensory exploration of artifacts and specimens from collections increased and extended visitor learning beyond the typical visual experience associated with the traditional gallery. Professionals dedicated to objects and collections hoped that the personal, hands-on experiences available in specially designed hands-on areas would spark interest in exhibitions outside of these spaces. Over the next four decades, the notion of discovery learning gained attention as a strategy for engaging learners.

The twenty-first-century museum continues to be perceived as a place of wonder where discovery is essential to the visitor experience and where many museums design spaces and exhibitions that include opportunities for handling objects. As new spaces appeared, the term *discovery* became prominent in their titles, showing a commitment to a certain type of learning experience that offers active, hands-on, exploratory learning. The list of museums embracing discovery learning is extensive and most often associated with natural history museums, science centers, and children's museums, but certainly extends beyond these institutions. At the Smithsonian Institution's National Museum of Natural History, families are invited to explore artifacts and specimens in Q'rius and Q'rius Jr. – a Discovery Room. The Cleveland Museum of Natural History advertises hands-on fun in the Smead Discovery Center, a space dedicated to intergenerational exploration, and the American Museum of Natural History in New York suggests that their Discovery Room is "an interactive gateway to the wonders of the Museum and a hands-on, behind-the-scenes look at its science" (American Museum of Natural History 2015).

As noted, discovery is not exclusively reserved for natural history and science museums, but is encouraged by art museums as well. The Nicolaysen Art Museum and Discovery Center in Casper, Wyoming, like many other art museums, is committed to visual arts and provides dedicated space for creative expression and exploration through art making as well as opportunities to experience art in galleries. There is little doubt that discovery is a hallmark of museum learning in many of today's museums.

Museum programs featuring discovery learning typically share common attributes, even though the content may differ from one institution to another. Visitors are invited to participate in hands-on, sensory experiences where they are free to select cultural artifacts or natural specimens as well as make personal decisions about their experiences. They also choose how they spend their time based on what captures their attention.

In discovery spaces, objects serve as a provocation, inviting the curiosity of the visitor. Museum educators or facilitators serve the public, available to support or scaffold learning by asking probing questions that focus attention or encourage further exploration. Written prompts posted in the physical space often provide guidance for visitors wanting more direct instruction. Although some spaces are designed for specific audiences, often children, most discovery rooms draw a broad audience from families with children of all ages to adults touring the museum independently. In any case, the opportunity for discovery can be found across a broad range of museums, inviting the curiosity of visitors.

Background on Curiosity

There is a long history of interest in curiosity as a human trait and attempts to define it. Early philosophers viewed curiosity broadly, Aristotle defining curiosity as "intrinsically motivated desire for information," while Cicero perceived it as an "innate love of learning and of knowledge … without the lure of any profit" (Loewenstein 1994, p. 76). William James (1899) wrote about curiosity suggesting that "in its higher, more intellectual form, the impulse toward completer knowledge takes the character of scientific or philosophical curiosity … Young children are possessed by curiosity about every new impression that assails them" (pp. 45–46).

Loewenstein, as a well-respected researcher and expert academic in the field of psychology, sheds light on the concept of curiosity, suggesting that incongruity, something out of place or unexpected, creates a desire to know and is triggered by "complexity, novelty, and surprise" (Jirout and Klahr 2012). This description aligns with Piaget's theory of assimilation and accommodation and his belief that individuals construct meaning about their world through interaction with the environment. "Piaget viewed curiosity as part of the process of assimilation, resulting from cognitive disequilibrium" (ibid., p. 6) where the child, curious from birth, responds to new or surprising experiences, discrepant from what she knows through experience. The child responds to the new phenomena by reconstructing internal cognitive schemas based on new information. According to Jirout and Klahr, curiosity is about "sense making" and can be depicted as "the threshold of desired environmental uncertainty that leads to exploratory behavior" (ibid., p. 5).

A child's natural curiosity is a catalyst for exploration and discovery, a process vital to learning. Researchers link this natural behavior to pleasure and play as understood in the context of neurodevelopment and suggest that "central to a child's healthy development is the opportunity to act on his natural curiosity" (Perry, Hogan, and Marlin 2000, p. 9). The experts describe a cycle that begins with play in its many forms, evolving in complexity and bringing pleasure to the child. Repetition leads to mastery and continued pleasure in accomplishment. With mastery comes a sense of comfort and a greater likelihood that the child "will explore, discover, master, and learn" (ibid., p. 9). The cycle begins with curiosity.

Curiosity is recognized as "an undeniably important aspect of children's cognitive development" (Jirout and Klahr 2012, p. 125). Interestingly, experts view this behavior as an indicator of school readiness (Kagan, Moore, and Bredekamp 1995) and believe it to be a more likely predictor of success than counting or reciting the alphabet (Jirout and Klahr 2012). Remarkably, there is no commonly agreed upon definition or measurement for curiosity, yet it remains a highly valued trait to nurture in young children.

Beyond the science of curiosity, there is enthusiastic consensus among early childhood educators that curiosity is critical to learning. This belief is widely accepted by organizations and individuals across the education field. In fact, the National Association for the Education of Young Children (NAEYC) includes the trait of curiosity in its standards describing best practice, suggesting that "children have varied opportunities to develop a sense of competence and positive attitudes toward learning, such as persistence, engagement, curiosity, and mastery" (NAEYC Criteria 2.B.04).

In exploration and in play, children show an amazing capacity to notice detail and see what others often miss. They are curious about their surroundings and create personal meaning that is unique to each child. Unlike adults, they are less likely to have preconceived notions that limit their ability to see. Looking at clouds, a young child sees a rabbit or a giant while the figures go unnoticed by others. At lunch time, a child looks beyond the reality of his half-eaten sandwich and imagines the shape to be a mouse or a hat, anything but the remnants of a sandwich. For children, imagination goes hand-in-hand with looking, which opens the mind to making associations with objects derived from past experience. Exploration stemming from a child's desire to know or fill an information gap contributes to cognitive growth and development. The vast majority of educators working with young children attribute behaviors of an exploratory nature to curiosity or an inquisitive mindset.

There are still gaps in research related to curiosity, specifically how it is defined and how it can be measured, and also a need to build on what is known to better understand the behavior and its impact on learning. The idea that curiosity can be influenced or nurtured is a belief that surfaces in the literature, and is a topic that deserves the attention of educators and parents.

Fostering Curiosity in Young Children

Conventional wisdom aligns with research to suggest that it is possible to build on children's natural inclination or curiosity to explore based on a few simple techniques. An important factor that influences a child's curiosity correlates with the actions of adult companions and their efforts to nurture a curious spirit, or inversely, squelch a child's desire to explore the unknown.

Modeling curiosity is a simple means for encouraging a child's curiosity. Adults who pay close attention to objects and details in their environment, pose questions about what they see, and express delight in discoveries, are modeling curiosity for little ones in their world. Modeling includes words and gestures that demonstrate an adult's genuine curiosity, but goes beyond actions and requires a risk-free environment for children to advance their own ideas and ask questions.

Consider a child's curiosity about a bird's nest found in the family's mailbox and the parent's response for fostering a desire to know. A conversation might begin with a parent's modeling of curiosity and a question that invites his child to be an active, thoughtful partner in conversation. *This is curious to find a bird's nest in the mailbox. Why do you think a bird would build a nest in our mailbox? What do you notice about this particular nest and where do you think the bird gathered materials for the nest? We see two eggs in the nest, but how many eggs do you think could fit? I wonder what the bird looks like that built this nest.* Questions are not intended to be linear or pre-planned, but rather responsive to a child's comments and observations. Simple, open-ended questions that encourage looking closely and thinking beyond what is seen, allow for a natural conversation to evolve. As Vygotsky suggests, all learning is socially mediated. Children learn from their social interactions and are quick to mimic the behaviors of others. When parents and teachers model curiosity, children gain a sense of comfort and are more likely to pursue their own interests and explore the unknown.

Research finds that inquiry, or the act of asking questions, is intrinsically linked to children's curiosity (Lind 1998; Martens 1999; Wilson 2002). Young children are apt to ask questions when they encounter something of interest, particularly something novel or unknown, and exhibit behaviors associated with curiosity. They look closely, use their senses to explore all aspects of an object, and seek connections to prior knowledge to make sense of their encounter. Although children are often the source of questions, the technique of inquiry is a useful tool for educators and parents as well. Asking probing questions is relevant to learning in a wide array of situations where children are engaged in problem-solving and information-seeking as part of play or exploration.

The science community, in particular, is invested in the idea of inquiry or questioning as a critical strategy for engaging young children in scientific thinking, and as a field recognizes the process of asking questions as a building block for scaffolding learning. Certain types of questions, referred to as productive questions, encourage children to look beyond their current thinking and consider other possibilities, remaining open for a wide range of alternatives (Martens 1999). Questions that invite children to think critically are favored over others, particularly those that "take a student forward in his or her thinking" (ibid., p. 25). The ideal is for children to become intellectual explorers seeking to solve problems and construct knowledge. Curiosity drives the exploration and the learning.

Similar values and techniques are found in research-based tools designed to assess the quality of early learning programs. For example, CLASS (Classroom Assessment Scoring System) offers educators a common metric to analyze quality of learning with indicators that include quality of feedback, questioning techniques encouraging higher-order thinking and problem-solving, classification and comparison, and language development. Whether in school settings or museum environments, children's natural inclinations as learners remain constant, and techniques that promote active learning, experimentation, and discovery support the natural curiosity of children as learners.

The environment is another critical factor in nurturing children's curiosity and is both a physical and social construct. The environment supports learning when it includes: (1) a variety of materials for hands-on exploration; (2) unstructured time that is controlled by the child; and (3) a social climate that promotes questioning, experimentation, and theory building without judgment by others (Wilson 2002). It is a place and culture that encourage exploration and experimentation, and trust children to engage in intellectual theory building. Learning for the young child is "an active enterprise" (Lind 1998, p. 3).

Supporting a child's curiosity is also linked to opportunity, particularly as it relates to play. Are children given ample opportunity to play and develop an internal sense of the world through external interactions with the environment? The research of Perry, Hogan, and Marlin (2000) offers a perspective that speaks to the value of play and its link to curiosity. "Curiosity, a neurobiological feature of many primates, drives exploratory play. Play can satisfy curiosity as the child explores her environment, thereby expanding her catalogue of experience. When the child explores, she discovers" (ibid., p. 9).

In addition to academic studies, professional organizations are advocates for young children and interested in developmental aspects of growth such as curiosity. Most recognized as a leader and advocate is the National Association for the Education of Young Children, but there are other credible organizations that bring a high level of expertise and knowledge to the field as well. For example, Zero to Three, an organization that "has a significant track record in turning the science of early development into helpful resources, practical tools and responsive policies for millions of parents, professionals, and policymakers" (website), offers tips for nurturing curiosity and suggests that listening to a child and supporting him in pursuing personal interests is fundamental to fostering curiosity. There are also on-line blogs that offer practical ideas for parents and teachers. One post suggests filling a small bag, designed for inquiry, with special tools to extend curiosity – magnifying glasses, colored pencils, small clipboard and paper, color swatches or paint chips from the paint store, simple objects related to the activity. These carefully selected items offer opportunities to enrich a young child's experience by providing a few special tools to investigate objects discovered on the walk, from acorns and pinecones to wildflowers and logs (Post by Kate Gribble, Childhood 101).

Children learn from their observations and interactions with others. When someone looks closely at a flower and wonders aloud about its vibrant color, its fluted petals, or its sweet fragrance, a child notes that behavior. When children are encouraged to interact with their environment, ask questions, or react to what they see, the likelihood that children will repeat these behaviors increases and curiosity becomes strengthened as a strategy for learning about the world.

Shining a Light on Objects

Research recognizes curiosity as a critical element in driving children's desire to know. In turn, exploration of the environment typically follows as a child seeks new information about those curiosities. Observations of young children lead parents and educators to similar conclusions that curiosity is a natural inclination in the early years that encourages a child to seek out information through a process of active exploration.

And while curiosity is understood as a natural behavior present from the earliest days of life, experts also believe that curiosity can be nurtured by the responses and modeling of adults as they interact with children, described in the research cited earlier. As children follow interests and curiosities, they rely on their sense of sight to notice similarities and differences to make meaning. In doing so, they often pay close attention to details to make distinctions among objects and better understand their world.

In addition to modeling curiosity, there are several interesting options for engaging young children in activities that encourage careful looking and at the same time allow pursuit of interests or curiosities. Photography and drawing are two such activities that have rich potential for children's learning.

Photography: A Focus on Objects

Photography is an art form that is common in our society, but one that is not always thought of in the context of young children. Engaging preschoolers and kindergartners in the art of photography develops important skills necessary for all aspects of learning, the most prominent being observation. When children take an active role in photography, they cultivate skills in noticing detail, making comparisons, recognizing relationships, expanding visual literacy, and building vocabulary to talk about what they see and their curiosities. In recent years, more and more educators, artists, and parents are becoming proponents of photography as an age-appropriate activity for children and see it as an experience that contributes to learning.

A basic premise essential to photography, the idea of learning to see, is an aptitude that is important for children. In photography, "seeing is the ability to observe what is before the photographer and visualize how it will appear in an image" (Krages 2005, p. 1). It speaks to the composition of a photograph or "the arrangement of visual elements so they agreeably present themselves when viewed as a whole" (ibid., p. 2). This includes balancing artistic elements such as light, line, shape, and space to create the aesthetic quality of the picture. Although this may be a sophisticated skill and one that is not expected for the novice, in truth, it begins with the ability to look carefully, noting details and relationships, an idea that is also important for cognitive growth and development of the child.

In the early years, learning to see is typically more about attention and making meaning from what is seen. The child takes in visual information and compares it to what is known, making meaning based upon prior knowledge. Through supportive interactions, children learn to focus on the details of an object, perhaps the shape, color, or design of a feather. Educators encourage children to look carefully as they interact with objects in their environment and then guide the looking by asking open-ended questions. *What words would you use to describe the feather? Let's look at two feathers and think about how they are the same and how they are different. What do you think?* With experience, children become more adept at noticing detail and actively engaging in the process of looking.

More and more, photography is viewed as appropriate for all ages, including young children. There are, in fact, a variety of websites and blogs that give parents and educators guidelines for introducing preschoolers to the art of photography. Clearly, preschoolers do not have the same capacity as practiced photographers who are able to create highly developed compositions with unique meaning, but they are capable of capturing some amazing images and understanding that the photograph is about something and tells a story. Success is a product of guiding behavior in the early stages and allowing children the freedom to explore the process once they develop some basic skills.

In the twenty-first century, cameras are accessible and easy to use whether in cell phones or iPads or as specific models designed especially for children. With technological advancements, high quality photographs are possible without expensive, fragile equipment and snapshots are easily viewed without cost before final selections are made, an amazing benefit of today's technology.

Young children are particularly interested in the magic of cameras. In the time that it takes to click the button, children are demanding to see the pictures. When given the chance, they are equally eager to take charge of the camera and become the photographer. There is a natural curiosity about the process that motivates children to become active participants.

Photography: From Theory to Practice

Introduce the idea of photography with a collection of photographs of familiar, everyday objects and places. Let the children look at the images and talk about what they see. Most children will know the difference between drawings and photographs, but a few simple questions will establish a foundation for the photography project. *What can you tell me about these pictures? How do you think these pictures were made? What would you need to do this? How is a photograph different from a painting or drawing? What might be the same?* Children's intuitive understanding guides their thinking and is supported by their general knowledge. A child's ability to express ideas through photography is often surprisingly sophisticated.

Once the idea of photography is introduced and there is a brief discussion about cameras, a simple demonstration showing how to take a picture is next. For budding photographers, the most important concept to learn is framing the picture: what you see through the camera lens is what is captured in the photograph. Some photographers talk about filling the frame, a concept that suggests the subject should fill the frame to eliminate distractions (Dickson 2015).

Precut mat frames found in local craft stores are inexpensive and perfect for practicing the art of framing (5" by 7" is a great size for little hands). Model the framing process for children by holding the cardboard frame in front of an interesting object and then view the object through the frame. Pretend to snap or click just as you would if taking a picture. Talk about what the picture will look like based on the framing experience and then give children frames for their own experimentation in the classroom, gallery, or outdoors. An exercise like this might seem trivial to adults, but it serves as a practical and meaningful lesson for young children. Take some time for children to talk about the pictures they frame with their pretend cameras.

After the framing exercise, let children use a real camera to take photographs of interesting objects, an experience sometimes referred to as a Discovery Walk. Children are most successful when there is a specific theme or idea to guide picture taking. Outdoor nature shots are always interesting and can be more focused by identifying a topic such as birds or leaves, but there are also interesting objects in classrooms and galleries – such as shoes, cups, chairs, or baskets – with endless possibilities. A theme focuses the children's attention and gives them something specific to look for in search of a great picture.

An important next step is reviewing the images with children, a task easily done on a screen or monitor. Teachers guide discussions so that children learn to be critical observers looking at their own photographs and those of their friends. *What is this picture about? Does it fill the frame? Is it interesting? What ideas do you have to make it better?* When teachers ask questions and encourage critical thinking, children become discriminating connoisseurs capable of discerning the quality of photographs.

PHOTOGRAPHY CAPTURES THE ATTENTION OF PRESCHOOLERS IN ATLANTA

As part of PNC's Grow Up Great grant, teaching artists from the High Museum of Art visited eleven preschool classrooms in Atlanta with children representing families with a low socio-economic status and introduced a program where 3-to-5-year-olds were encouraged to use cameras, and teachers were introduced to strategies to integrate photography into daily classroom routines. Over the course of a semester, students and teachers became comfortable with the camera (a Canon Powershot D20, chosen for its sturdiness and simple functionality) and began using it to document their friendships, classroom work, objects that were particularly important to them, and the natural world they encountered every day.

According to Kristen Buckley, the Early Childhood Program Manager, in one interesting case, a class of preschoolers embarked on a study of nature with a specific interest in trees. Teachers and teaching artists asked children to use the camera on a tree scavenger hunt in the school's playground. An exercise that began as a way to demonstrate close observation morphed into an activity that changed the way the students interacted with the natural world. Instead of simply looking for bark, acorns, pinecones, leaves, trunks, and branches of trees, the children manipulated these elements in new ways, creating artful displays of leaves and then photographing them, or snapping a photograph of a friend rubbing the bark of a tree in a gesture of friendship and recognition. The children printed photographs, created titles for each image, and produced a book about different types of trees (Figures 5.1–5.3). The fact that students used their art to create a field guide points to the fertile potential that photography offers young children and their teachers as a tool for documentation, reflection, and reference throughout the year.

Curiosity is often a driving force in moving a project like this forward. The novelty of taking photographs appeals to young children. Not only do children enjoy the process, but they also are excited about the product. Through the excitement, children develop skills in noticing detail, learn to see the world literally and figuratively through a different lens, and expand abilities and interests. Favorite photographs are treasured and in some cases represent the first step in collecting.

As educators and parents introduce this somewhat novel approach, it is important to recognize that this strategy, like all other successful strategies, focuses on the child. It is also helpful to remember that children enjoy repetition and willingly repeat actions again and again, which fits well with the idea that practice is essential to a child's comfort and success. As novice photographers, children need time and practice to hone their skills whether at home, in a museum, or at preschool. Practice, practice, practice is the mantra to follow!

68 Learning to Look at Objects

FIGURE 5.1 Nature: Stackable Leaves
Source: Preschooler, PNC Grow Up Great/The Alliance Theatre

FIGURE 5.2 Nature: I See a Nest
Source: Preschooler, PNC Grow Up Great/The Alliance Theatre

Learning to Look at Objects 69

FIGURE 5.3 Nature: A Bug Lives Here
Source: Preschooler, PNC Grow Up Great/The Alliance Theatre

Drawing with Young Children: Cultivating Attention to Detail

Drawing is a technique typically associated with visual arts and perceived as an art form that develops over time and with practice. It is a universal experience that appeals to all ages, but often captures the attention of the very young as they attempt to mimic the behavior of adults in their environment, experimenting with pencils, pens, markers, and other interesting writing tools.

For the young child, it is the wonder and awe of marks magically appearing on paper, or to the chagrin of adults, on other surfaces, without concern for a particular product or representation. A toddler has little interest in recreating an object that reflects reality, but rather is enamored with the process of drawing and making marks. It is the action that stimulates the child and motivates further efforts.

As cognitive abilities develop and children demonstrate greater flexibility and control of small motor skills needed to manipulate writing tools, the act of drawing begins to shift from being exclusively about process to a greater focus on representation. This desire to recreate a specific object or event through drawing happens earlier in development for some, while for others, the focus on process continues until a later time. What is important to remember is that it cannot be described as one size fits all.

Children's drawings stem from imagination, memories from past experience, or connections to the here and now. As an art form, drawing taps into the creativity of the child with an emphasis on self-expression. With maturation, children's abilities to draw and their interest in things represented in the world increase and they learn to add more and more detail to their drawings, from the spikes and protective plates of a stegosaurus to the fingers and toes of a human being. Drawing can be open-ended and imaginative or can focus attention on recreating a graphic representation of objects from the environment. There are merits to both types of drawing. When children demonstrate more refined small motor dexterity and show an interest in representing ideas on paper, the time is right to introduce drawing as a technique for learning in galleries or classrooms.

> **DRAWING: AN EVOLVING EXPERIENCE FOR YOUNG CHILDREN**
>
> Drawing is defined in childhood as stages of development, beginning with scribbling or the kinesthetic phase, usually at about 15 months of age, which refers to the period where random marks are plentiful and action is the most salient feature for the child. Scribbling is followed by representational drawing, a more intentional phase where children are more deliberate in their marks, initially circles and purposeful lines, with more focus on the symbolic representation of each. Children typically enter this phase at about 3–4 years of age (Di Leo 1980). A child's desire to represent objects as they are in the real world follows naturally, at different times for different children.

In the museum world, there are a variety of programs that encourage visitors to draw or sketch. For some, the terms *drawing* and *sketching* are seemingly interchangeable, while for others, they represent nuanced differences. For those who see nuanced differences, drawing typically represents a more finished product whereas sketching is viewed as a preliminary action, more quickly accomplished to capture the essence of the object. Whether referring to drawing or sketching, the National Gallery of Art in Washington, DC, similar to many other museums, sees value in this type of experience. "Sketching encourages us, regardless of age or ability, to slow down, to look carefully, and to connect with works of art. It allows us time to see more and experience works of art through a different lens" (National Gallery of Art website 2017).

Drawing as a technique or skill, particularly when the aim is to replicate what is visible at the moment, requires careful looking and attention to detail. Cultivating a child's ability to observe contributes to patterns of learning across multiple domains, but is particularly critical to the sciences. Through some simple steps, educators can nurture a child's ability to observe and notice details, all while engaging in an age-appropriate experience.

Typical activities in classrooms or galleries can incorporate drawing and are likely to interest children when they have choice in the subject of the drawing. With the cup collection, each child chooses a cup of his choice. In other drawing experiences, the choices can be broader. *Find an interesting object in the outdoor garden. Look at the baskets in the art gallery and choose one that you would like to draw. Look at the creatures in the aquarium and decide which one is most interesting, then draw that specimen.* By expanding the depth and breadth of drawing lessons or activities, children will be able to follow their own interests and curiosities.

> **A DRAWING ACTIVITY FOR CHILDREN**
>
> Imagine a collection of cups of different sizes and shapes, each with unique patterns and colors, as a starting point for a children's experience in careful looking. Ask the children to look closely at the collection and then initiate a conversation with an open-ended question as a prompt. *What do you notice about the objects?* The responses will connect to what children see, with some children noticing greater detail than others. This process encourages children to learn from one another and focus attention on details they might have missed.
>
> Guided looking is also important in the opening minutes of the children's activity. Each child selects one cup from the collection, ultimately with the task of drawing the object. Children are asked to pay attention to details of their object and are guided in the process of looking closely. A few simple questions, intended as prompts for thinking, encourage children to look closely at their objects. *Do you think that all cups are the same? Think about the shape of your cup. Do you see straight lines or curved lines? Does your cup have a handle, and if so, what is its shape? Is there a design or picture on your cup, and if so, what details do you notice that make it special? What do you notice about the colors of your cup?* Encourage the children to look at all parts of their cup – closely at the top part of their cup, then the bottom, and finally the middle. Remind the group that each cup in the collection is different and that details are important in their drawings.
>
> Now the children are ready to draw and incorporate details that reflect reality. As children near completion of their drawings, ask them to look again at their cups to see if they notice any other details that might be missing. The final step is to have children display their drawings and objects, and then talk about their drawings.
>
> An extension of this activity focuses more on imagination. Have cutouts of different styles of cups with a variety of sizes and shapes as the background for the activity or invite children to draw and cut out a cup shape of their own. Encourage children to think about a design or pattern for their cup and then provide colored pencils or markers for the actual artistic endeavor.

Drawing is an experience that has a range of possibilities for engaging children. It is also a valued activity in museums and schools. As the Getty Museum blog suggests, "Whether drawing to express yourself, to discover rich patterns or details in art, or to create lasting memories of being with an object or view, drawing trains the hand, eye, and mind – all while relaxing you!" (Zaluski 2017).

Conclusion

Discovery learning is a natural fit for the young learner, whether at home, in school, or at the museum. It is an active approach to learning that offers a range of unique opportunities that fit well with the way that children learn. That spirit of discovery stems from an innate sense of curiosity. In a world that is new and exciting, it is understandable that a child would be inquisitive. Research offers insight into this characteristic and recognizes its significance for early learning and its relationship to discovery. Experts also suggest that this natural phenomenon that we understand as curiosity is a trait or behavior that can be nurtured in the early years.

Whether thinking about the informal museum environment or the more formal school setting, it is important to plan museum programs and classroom activities in light of current research. Opportunities to engage young visitors broaden as educators look to one another for examples of success. Photography and drawing as early experiences are two such examples that encourage careful looking and build a foundation for future learning. Not only are children actively engaged in the learning process, but they are making choices and developing critical skills while having fun.

6

CURIOSITY AND COLLECTIONS: A CHILD'S PERSPECTIVE

> I think, at a child's birth, if a mother could ask a fairy godmother to endow it with the most useful gift, that gift should be curiosity.
>
> Eleanor Roosevelt

Children and Collecting

A Natural Desire to Explore and Collect

Young children are naturally curious about their world, a disposition that begins at a very early age. As noted by Eleanor Roosevelt, curiosity is an attribute that she considers to be a gift and something that every child deserves. This gift of curiosity, or innate desire to know, leads to interaction with the environment and exploration through the senses. Research confirms that "very young children are active agents of their own concept development" (National Research Council 2000, pp. 79–80) and "depend on will, ingenuity, and effort to enhance their learning" (ibid., p. 83). And so begins the story of curiosity and the journey of learning.

Every object is new to a child upon first encounter. And even though a child's interest and motivation to know are in place at birth, knowledge of the world and the objects that fill the space is unknown until some encounter introduces clues about what it is and how it might be used. Whether it's a lost button under mother's desk, the cat's water bowl on the kitchen floor, or a coaster on a coffee table, objects have little meaning for a child until they are understood in context. What might be perceived by an adult as a seemingly commonplace object with little appeal is viewed with fascination by a toddler.

The coaster found by chance on the coffee table is scrutinized and explored using every sense. The toddler absorbs physical attributes of the object by looking closely, listening for possible sounds, and then using additional senses of touch, taste, and smell to learn more. Predictably, the toddler bangs the coaster on the table, captivated by the sounds. In this process of learning, coasters are stacked, placed in lines, and carried around the room. They are positioned in open spaces, sometimes hidden from view, and later retrieved for other purposes. It is not until a child sees someone in the home repeatedly placing a glass on the coaster that the object is viewed in context and defined for its intended purpose. For a young child, a simple coaster becomes many things in the process of exploration.

This fascination with objects likely relates to a child's natural curiosity and a desire to know, but other factors could be in play as well. Bright red pots capture a child's attention and pop in contrast to other things in the room. A mirror that reflects light or even shiny casters attached to the legs of a chair draw a young child's attention. Leaves from an indoor plant, blowing in the breeze from an open window, are certain to be of interest to an exploring baby or toddler. It might simply be a child's access to an object that leads to exploration. Bright colors, shiny surfaces, movement, and even sounds can increase attention and curiosity. A young child quickly discovers that treasures abound in the surrounding environment.

The Earliest Form of Collecting

Natural curiosity, and interest in the things of the world, continue as a young child becomes mobile and ventures into new environments. Found objects, from indoor and outdoor spaces, are examined closely and find their way into pockets, sometimes with little thought about the actual object and its inherent value or interest. This stash of found objects is dismissed from memory without a second thought by some little ones, while others save and return to the collection at a later time for deeper exploration. This is the beginning of collecting, an action that in its earliest stages is often more about the process than the actual objects. A time will come when the child is intentional in what he collects with decisions based on a specific interest or passion. These early collections may at times be tucked away and given little thought or, in some cases, explored in play.

Children interact with objects in many different ways, depending on developmental level. In play, a young toddler fills a box with different types of blocks, and then dumps them only to refill the container. The choice of objects is immaterial at this stage of play; it is the process of filling, dumping, and refilling that dominates the child's activities. This type of play might be construed broadly as an early stage in collecting, primarily in the context of gathering.

With time, objects become important and more specific in collecting and in play. Each box or container is filled with objects having common attributes, blocks in one container, beads in another, and pegs in yet another. In imaginative play, a child pretends that each container holds a different type of candy or she may instead focus only on the process of matching objects with similar attributes of shape. A child's natural tendency to create meaning is visible in the child's ability "to set goals, plan, and revise" and apply strategies to "assemble and organize material" (National Research Council 2000, p. 80). Actions reflect a process that is thoughtful and intentional.

This example of gathering and sorting demonstrates a child's inclination to make sense of the world by comparing physical attributes of objects in the environment, focusing primarily on similarities and differences. Knowledge gleaned from sensory experience is applied in play when children sort, order, and classify objects as with the blocks, beads, and pegs. And while this is a common activity fostered in early childhood classrooms, the tendency arises naturally in everyday life.

Personal Interests as Inspiration for Collections

Any object has the potential to spark a child's interest, and in time, lead to collecting. Different children are drawn to different objects, with choices reflecting a personality or preferences that build incrementally. Dewey recognized the significance of children's interests and suggested that they "represent dawning capacities" (Dewey 1897, p. 80), but how do these dawning capacities or interests develop for young children? What is it that ignites a particular passion for collecting, particularly for someone of a young age? Is 3-year-old Jason's fascination with animals linked to his weekly visits to the community zoo as a young toddler? Is Marco's obsession with fire engines connected to the rescue squad vehicles visible in his neighborhood? Is Margo's desire to collect bugs a reflection of her father's work as an entomologist? While a pivotal experience or encounter that sparks interest may go unnoticed, it is likely that seeds are planted in ordinary moments of life, some of which go far beyond casual curiosity and may, at some time, play an important role in the future.

Collections can be inspired by a single object that a child sees in his environment; certainly shells on the beach or rocks at the park reflect this idea. Family collections, from antique cooking tools displayed on the kitchen wall to a collection of postcards from museum shops or family travels, open the door for a child's interest to develop (Figure 6.1). Children's books and videos are also places where little ones are exposed to objects and experiences; some objects gain prominence in a child's play and at times lead to collecting. Dewey's belief that experience is critical to a child's growth, and also an impetus for the personal construction of knowledge, sheds light on why children collect.

Collecting takes on new meaning when special interests enter into the way a child interacts with his world, showing preferences and making choices. A walk on the beach becomes an opportunity to collect shells or colored sea glass for one young collector while another child searches far and wide for cats, from Beanie Baby kittens to ceramic felines. One preschooler is emphatic in her search for rocks, gathering them upon every outing, yet frequently losing interest in the objects collected. This lack of interest does not seem to impact her desire to find rocks in future excursions, but the process of collecting seems to be the primary incentive for her activity.

For some, every object related to the child's passion becomes part of the collection. Other children are, however, more discriminating in their choice of objects. As interests develop, children begin to seek out objects related to that

76 Curiosity and Collections

FIGURE 6.1 Young toddler curious about a collection of postcards
Source: Photograph by Alyson Williams.

interest; ultimately, objects representing personal interests become prevalent in the child's play, language development, and social interaction. Wesley talks about trains, plays with trains, selects *Freight Train* (Donald Crews 1978) for his bedtime story, and uses every opportunity to look and listen for trains when out in the neighborhood. What was once a simple attraction can now be considered a true passion!

Personal experiences become the inspiration or foundation for collecting. Social interactions introduce children to family treasures collected over time, just as family visits to museums, zoos, nature centers, or other cultural institutions at times inspire personal interests. It is often difficult to know what sparks interest for a particular child, but a child's curiosity becomes evident in his everyday activities.

COLLECTING NATIONALS' MEMORABILIA

Henry is an avid collector of all things Nationals (i.e. the Washington Nationals baseball team), an interest that developed before the age of 3. His family's dedication to the team as season ticket holders defined them as ardent fans, a role that Henry fully embraced. Regular visits to the ballpark provided opportunities for Henry to collect tickets, brochures, programs, photographs, and of course, special giveaways such as Nationals' bobble heads. Henry's love of

> baseball is present in his collection of Nationals' memorabilia, but goes beyond his cherished team to other teams in the league with his collection of baseball cards. This collection is special to Henry because of his love of baseball, but also holds a place of pride in his life as a hobby shared with his father who began collecting baseball cards as a young child.

Collections on Display

Children's environments, at home and at school, are places filled with objects and often include those specifically designed for play, from building blocks of different types to puppets, dolls, trucks, books, and puzzles. A snapshot of one play space is likely similar to many others, at least for children fortunate enough to have this type of home or school environment. By looking closely at the space and its contents, it's often possible to identify a child's interests, revealed by the specific objects collected.

A well-organized play space, especially in preschool settings, has much in common with formally displayed collections with each area organized by theme: blocks grouped by type in open containers, children's books on shelves, and props for pretend play (such as dishes or costumes) in baskets. The science center boasts a collection of natural materials from leaves and twigs to rocks and bark, all materials from the outdoor environment. Each collection is organized around a common theme or contains objects with similar attributes.

When parents and teachers respect children's interests, the environment begins to reflect the individual child or group. This is true for an individual child or for preschoolers in a classroom. Walk into Henry's room and there is no doubt that he loves the Nationals. Morgan's interest in nature is apparent in her informal collections of rocks, shells, sticks, and leaves. Excitement about birds is evident in Emma's preschool classroom, a space filled with collections of nests, feathers, and children's drawings of different types of birds. It's easy to see what appeals to children in each of these examples.

Objects are collected, stored, and displayed in many different ways. The old-fashioned cigar box is a relic of the past, and is replaced today by plastic containers or decorative cardboard boxes appropriate for storing precious treasures. For some preschoolers, trinkets are hidden away while other children display objects for all to see. Stephen's miniature dinosaurs are arranged neatly on a bedroom shelf while Mark's bottle caps are clustered in a small box. The inclination to collect and the decision regarding display of objects differ with each child.

Collections in the Classroom in Formal Learning Environments

Collecting is not reserved exclusively for the informal experiences that take place at home, but is also present in more formal preschool, kindergarten, and early elementary classrooms, with collections taking center stage in museum schools like the Smithsonian Early Enrichment Center (SEEC) and the Opal School at the Portland Children's Museum. Educators use objects and collections to engage students and make abstract ideas concrete.

SEEC, the Smithsonian's museum-based lab school, has a history of integrating collecting into learning experiences in classrooms. Kindergartners become student curators and plan, organize, and create classroom exhibitions based on personal collections that are amazingly diverse and range from snow globes to insects. Students are comfortable in their knowledge of collecting, recognize that museums are repositories for collections, and understand that artifacts from collections are displayed in exhibitions. The concept of collecting has meaning in their personal world and is understood as fundamental to museums' work. SEEC's preschoolers, primarily 3- and 4-year-old children, collaborate on curriculum-related collections to document and share their learning with classmates, parents, and community members. A collection of buttons is displayed during a study of clothing and different types of fasteners. Feathers, nests, eggs, and birdhouses will be included in a classroom exhibition related to a study of birds and their habitats. Handcrafted clay pots of different shapes, created by children, are arranged to complement the story of Demi's (1996) *The Empty Pot*. Collections are tangible representations of ideas explored in the early learning environments of the Smithsonian's lab school and have been a hallmark of the program for many years.

Collections are also on display at the Opal School in Portland, Oregon, a program "inspired by the work of early childhood schools of Reggio Emilia, Italy" (Portland Children's Museum 2015), but they also serve an important purpose in sparking the interest of children as they construct, create, and develop stories. A basket of sparkly things inspires students to add new ideas, include more detail in drawings, or extend thinking when writing a story or creating a collage. In Opal School classrooms, collections are thought of as a teaching tool and envisioned as an opportunity to uncover hidden ideas.

Not only are collections valued, but the individual object is also recognized as a source of stories. Objects wake up connections or serve as a catalyst for thinking and creating. It is the everyday object, in many cases, those found in nature, receiving attention from Opal students and teachers. It is not uncommon to see children collecting twigs or stones from the outdoor play space and quietly placing them in a pocket for later analysis or play. Children's unique interests are valued and respected, much like the objects that they collect. Respect is central to the school's philosophy.

One child discovers an acorn beneath an oak tree, looking closely at the color, shape, size, and textures of the nut, using a range of senses to observe and make meaning. Observation is a valued skill that children practice at Opal School, so noticing details comes naturally. It is not until that same child finds another acorn that she begins to compare the characteristics of the two objects and notices details formerly missed. One acorn, then two, quickly become a collection. Each acorn is valued for its unique features while also seen in comparison to others. In play, acorns are ordered by size from the smallest to the largest, and at another time, grouped by another prominent feature, acorns with a cap and those without. With a little imagination, a subset of the collection takes on new meaning and is viewed as a family with each acorn identified for a specific role (i.e. mother, father, child, pet, etc.). The collection is shared with others in the classroom and becomes integrated into other class projects.

Creativity and artistic expression are highly valued attributes and visible in the imaginative endeavors of children working in Opal School classrooms where natural materials are gathered and sorted into containers for artistic experimentation, and are, in essence, collections of natural objects. Projects reflect student learning, and through classroom displays, communicate that learning to others. Objects and collections take pride of place in Opal School where respect for the child and the environment is paramount.

It is not only museum schools that value collections. Palm Beach Day Academy (PBDA), an independent school in West Palm Beach, Florida, has an established culture of teaching with objects and integrating collections into classroom learning. The first grade teachers integrate collections into every aspect of curriculum throughout the year and acknowledge the power of the object in teaching.

Programs that include collections exist in schools from a variety of countries and cultures. An interesting model from Canada is gaining international attention for its emphasis on nature education with collecting as a component of the curriculum. Commonly termed *forest schools*, programs representing this growing trend dedicate their time to learning math, science, social studies, and language arts through hands-on exploration in a natural environment. Children collect objects such as leaves, sticks, pine cones, rocks, and other specimens as a source of information and use everyday objects from nature to make sense of their world and to tell stories. Collections are a natural part of the curriculum.

In a more traditional elementary school, it is not uncommon to see teachers using objects or collections to introduce ideas or illustrate concepts. For some, the idea of collections may be intentionally embedded in teaching strategies; others might use collections of objects, but may not think about their practice in the context of collecting and collections. What is evident is the value of objects and collections in children's learning.

Display is part of the collecting process in formal and informal environments, and valued in different ways by different children. Joy comes from the selection and collection of specific objects, but is also found in the interaction or play with those carefully chosen treasures. The visual presence, and for some children, arranging the valued objects, are as important as the collecting. What is compelling for one child as a collector may be less important for another. Each child relates to the idea of collecting and collections in a unique way.

The desire to collect and share enthusiasm for objects of interest exists from an early age. Educators from formal and informal settings integrating this knowledge into their work in designing curriculum and developing programs will be building on natural inclinations of children as collectors, and as a result, create strong, meaningful experiences for the young.

Children's Literature: Exploring the Idea of Collecting and Collections

Children learn about their world through a wide range of experiences. They are drawn to the physical things of the environment and exhibit a desire to explore through their senses. Theorists, researchers, and educators acknowledge the role of objects in learning, but they also understand that children learn through narrative and storytelling.

Children's books, written and illustrated specifically with the young child in mind, introduce and explain new concepts and build important skills. They put children's lived experiences into words and illustrations, bringing new perspectives to extend understanding of everyday actions. Among professionals, there is little quarrel about the value of books and the contribution that reading makes to cognitive and social development. "According to the National Center for Education Statistics (NCES), a division of the U.S. Department of Education, children who are read to at home enjoy a substantial advantage over children who are not" (National Education Association 2015). Books make a difference in how children learn about and understand their world.

A vast array of books can be found in libraries, schools, and bookstores in most communities, offering easy access to children's literature for families. Media campaigns touting the importance of literacy and its value in the early years are reaching parents across most socio-economic groups and sharing an important message about the value of books. Further information is available through position papers written by professional organizations such as the National Association for the Education of Young Children (NAEYC) and the International Reading Association (IRA) to inform readers of benefits and share research findings to encourage reading to young children from the earliest days of life. Certainly for educators, but also for many families, the idea of reading in the early years is an accepted norm.

In formal programs, the practice of reading is highly valued by early childhood educators where story time is an expected activity in every preschool classroom of quality. Children's books are rich in language and visual art; they offer opportunities to explore abstract concepts, consider new ideas, and discover imaginary places. A child's world is enriched by children's stories and poetry.

There is a lovely intersection of story and object when children's authors explore the concept of collections. *The Room of Wonder* by Sergio Ruzzier recounts the story of Pius, the pack rat, and his zest for collecting objects from his environment, from twisted twigs and interesting leaves to objects abandoned or lost. Pius exhibits his treasures on shelves in the Room of Wonders, including his most beloved object, a small gray pebble. Pius' friends, however, are perplexed by his interest in the pebble because it is so ordinary. Through this book, children learn about collecting and exhibiting objects, and come to understand that interests differ with each individual.

What is ordinary for one individual seems extraordinary to another. Most important is the message of personal connection to the objects collected.

Author I.C. Springman explores the idea of collecting in *More*, a story that begins with a magpie who has nothing and slowly collects objects one by one, adding more and more to his nest until he has way too much (Springman 2012). A crisis leads to the realization that less is more. Although the magpie's collection is somewhat random, the bird clearly is a collector. *More* opens a conversation about what it means to collect.

But the magpie is not the only bird interested in collecting. Cynthia DeFelice's *Clever Crow* brings meaning to the idea of collecting through a story of a black crow who loves "nickels, quarters, diamond rings" and other shiny things, causing problems for a neighboring family (DeFelice 1998). Luckily, young Emma recognizes Crow's passion and uses a ball of shiny gum wrappers from her box of treasures to trick the bird and retrieve shiny keys from Crow's possession, solving the family dilemma. Young children easily see that Crow likes shiny things and collects these objects for himself. Collections appear in the story with Emma's special treasures hidden in a box beneath her bed as well as the stolen stash in Crow's nest. *Clever Crow* offers a wonderful opportunity to talk about what it means to collect and the characteristics of a collection.

For some children, collections are tied to specific objects, such as shells or rocks, while for others collecting is based on a broader theme, such as Crow's shiny things. Eve Bunting explores collecting from a thematic perspective by sharing a child's love of nature in *Anna's Table* (Bunting 2003). Anna collects unusual objects that include the remnants of creatures such as a Fiddler crab, feathers, a shark's tooth, and dusty nests; every object represents nature. Anna finds beauty and intrigue in all things natural and celebrates her treasures by displaying them on a small table selected specifically for this purpose. *Anna's Table* offers an opportunity to discuss different types of collections and the idea of display.

So while Anna celebrates nature broadly, Rhoda is drawn to one specific aspect of the natural world, rocks. *Rhoda's Rock Hunt* (Molly Beth Griffen 2014) follows Rhoda on a hike through the north woods where she collects rocks. "Rhoda loved ROCKS. Smooth rocks and bumpy rocks and sparkly rocks and stripy rocks and rocks shaped like hearts and hats and horns" (ibid.). Descriptions of various rocks help the reader think about the many attributes of a single object and learn about the complexity of the world. A rock is more than a rock, and every rock is unique. This concept of complexity can be applied to most collections and is useful in talking with a child about her collection. *What is it that you like about this rock? How is this rock different from another rock?* By learning about attributes or defining characteristics of objects, children are able to sort, organize, and classify objects in their collections. *Let's sort the rocks into groups by color. Look at the size of each rock and place rocks in order from largest to smallest.* The process of collecting is engaging for most children, but the conversation that emerges through interacting with personal collections can be a powerful opportunity for children to express their ideas and develop new understandings.

This affinity for nature is common among young children. A basket of pine cones attracts a toddler's attention and for some leads to the careful examination of each individual pine cone. Backyard leaves and twigs are carried around and incorporated into play. Stones are collected and placed in lines along the edge of a sidewalk. There is a wealth of opportunity in nature's backyard.

But children also show interest in everyday objects found in the home. *Hannah's Collections* (Marthe Jocelyn 2000) is a story about a young girl who loves to collect, and considers every object a treasure. She collects buttons, Popsicle sticks, barrettes, plastic rings, coins, stamps, dolls, erasers, keys, clothes pins, and paper clips as well as shells, leaves, feathers, and more. Hannah playfully interacts with her collections, arranging the Popsicle sticks in patterns by crisscrossing sticks or placing them in different directions or sorting the buttons by size, shape, and color. Her fascination with objects and love of collecting carry over into other day-to-day activities.

A particular interest in collections does not always begin with the child, but may come from experiencing another person's collection. *The Button Box* (Margarette S. Reid 1990) tells the story of a young boy's discovery of his grandmother's box of buttons and the joy they experience together. The pair carefully examines buttons, finding those with identical designs or grouping objects by color, size, or shape. They imagine military men wearing buttons designed with eagles, flags, or anchors and pretend that sparkly buttons adorned the clothing of movie stars, kings, and queens. They find that buttons are made of many different materials and have various textures. An afternoon with grandma's collection sparks many discoveries, but promises more for future visits. This story resonates with children and adults alike who have experienced something similar with a beloved family member.

Personal collections are likely to be perceived by children as treasures, no matter how uninteresting or insignificant the objects may seem to someone else. *Treasures of the Heart* (Alice Ann Miller 2003) reminds us how important it is to respect the interests of children and realize that everyday trinkets are often "heartfelt memories" that have individual meaning. Sharing in a child's joy is an experience that demonstrates respect and understanding.

There are many beautiful children's books available today that provide opportunities to explore the idea of collecting and collections. Each has a special message, but most resonate with children for the passion and excitement shared for objects.

Conclusion

Collecting is a natural inclination for young children and an activity that continues throughout life. It's important to understand that children are unique in their interests and to respect the choices that are represented in things collected. For most children, collecting is less about things that come from stores, but rather about objects found in natural interactions with the world. We need only think about Pius' ordinary pebble to remember that the worth or value of an object comes from the heart.

7

OBJECT LESSONS INSPIRED BY HISTORY MUSEUMS AND HISTORIC HOMES

> The eye can see more in a minute than a half hour's descriptive reading will tell. Giving a child a chance to see and handle the things about which they study is not only the greatest timesaver, but [also] the most effective way of giving an absolutely correct impression.
>
> Levi W. Mengel, Reading Public Museum, in Findlay and Perricone (2009)

Introduction

Museums are trusted institutions that seek knowledge and understanding through a study of objects. This reliance on objects as a source of information is important not only in museums, but, as Levi Mengel suggests, critical to a child's ability to gain "an absolutely correct impression." As an advocate for sensory exploration of objects, Mengel maintained that an experience of sight or touch, for example, far outweighs any learning that is derived from words alone, particularly for the young. This connection to objects suggests that history museums, like others, deserve consideration as a place of learning for children.

In the twenty-first century, history museums and historical sites are welcoming young children to their galleries in greater numbers than ever before and are recognized for the rich opportunities they offer children to learn core principles relevant to understanding history. Even at a young age, the idea of *past and present* is part of a young child's personal life experience. Early exposure to the concept of *then and now* holds relevance for an introduction to history and with guidance from adults is ultimately understood as everything that has already happened, at least in the minds of children. In fact, these are the exact words of a 5-year-old describing the term *history*.

Children also recognize *change over time* as something that occurs in the real world, making this discovery when comparing objects or places from the past with those familiar in their own lives, a process that starts to shape a child's mental constructs defining history. An old-fashioned bicycle is distinct from a child's experience with bicycles, yet the historic artifact retains enough similar features for instant recognition by a child. It is easy to see that today's object represents a change from the object of the past.

Historical institutions also introduce preschoolers and kindergartners to specific people and events that make up the fabric of society. And although chronological understanding is not yet developed in a sense required for the study of history, familiarity with simple stories about important figures, like Thomas Jefferson or Rosa Parks, have meaning for children independent of other historical events, and later are integrated into appropriate time periods that contribute to more sophisticated grasp of time and history. Early experiences are the building blocks for a future understanding of history yet also have meaning independent of broader historical context.

Most museums have the potential to engage children, even when exhibitions are not conceived of with the young visitor in mind. In these cases, the objectives of the curatorial team are in all probability beyond the scope of a typical preschooler, but within the exhibition, there are likely objects that may be diamonds in the rough, hidden gems that seem ordinary at first glance, but take on new meaning when given careful thought and viewed through the eyes of a child. To appeal to the young mind, an approach that privileges the senses is key.

The idea of sensory-rich learning has a long history, yet applies equally to learning in the twenty-first century. Levi Mengel, "the founder and visionary behind the Reading Public Museum" (Findlay & Perricone 2009, p. 11) and its museum school (1908), understood that sensory-rich experiences provide the best approach for learning where children are likely to reach the most accurate understanding, while also gaining knowledge and developing "the habit of attention and close observation" (ibid., p. 12). It is widely recognized that museums offer exceptional opportunities for children to acquire knowledge through their senses, particularly in the twenty-first century where museums represent rich visual experiences that are increasingly complemented by tactile and auditory experiences.

Think about an historic home, replete with art and artifacts from centuries past. The history of the home and its family may not necessarily have great appeal to the typical four- or five-year-old, but individual objects within the home afford great possibility for engaging the young if thoughtfully presented. Consider the Great Clock at the entrance of Monticello, an invention of Thomas Jefferson that captures the attention of visitors of all ages, or Mount Vernon's house bell at the home of George Washington with its unique design and purpose. A child's familiarity with everyday objects, as simple as a clock or bell, creates a point of departure for investigating historical artifacts housed in the homes of people from the past.

History Museums and Historic Homes

The object lessons suggested for history museums and historic homes are intended to reflect practices that may easily be applicable to a wide range of historic environments. At the same time, each is inspired by a particular institution or collection. These lessons are not intended to be highly structured, but rather a framework for exploring ideas in a manner that is relevant to young visitors. Because of the broad topics, museum educators can readily adapt ideas to different types of collections to include the treasured homes of historic figures as well as the less well-known dwellings held close to the heart by small communities.

Object Lesson 1 History

The first lesson is designed around the concept of keys, objects that are ubiquitous in today's society and familiar to children, yet also significant in centuries past. A key, like many other objects, can serve as a tangible catalyst for stories of our ancestors and engage young children in making meaningful connections between today and the past.

> ### OBJECT LESSON: UNLOCKING THE MYSTERIES OF THE PAST IN HISTORIC HOMES: MONTPELIER
>
> MONTPELIER was home to President James Madison, Father of the Constitution and Architect of the Bill of Rights, and Dolley Madison, America's first "First Lady." The Montpelier estate features the mansion, garden, historic buildings, exhibits, archaeological sites, and forests trails.
>
> *Montpelier 2016*
>
> ### Background and Core Strategies
>
> Young children construct meaning about their world by making associations between the familiar and unfamiliar. This often begins with curiosity and a child's desire to understand the discrepancies that arise when comparing similar, yet distinctly different objects or experiences. A high society hat from the 1920s is recognized immediately as a hat, but is clearly understood as different from most hats in a child's experience. Curiosity drives the process of exploration and encourages attention to discreet details or features of objects both familiar and unfamiliar.
>
> In his texts, Piaget describes this natural inclination to make associations as a process of assimilation and accommodation where mental constructs are created through experience and serve as a source of comparison for new encounters. Information gathered through experience is considered in light of what is already known. If there are inconsistencies between the established mental construct and the new experience, the new information is integrated and ultimately contributes to the modification of the internal construct to achieve what Piaget construes as a state of equilibrium.

This process of constructing meaning is addressed as a fundamental concept in constructivist learning theory. Prior knowledge, a product of past experience, is considered an essential building block for gaining new knowledge. Theorists John Dewey, Lev Vygotsky, Jean Piaget, Jerome Bruner, and others understood that experience combined with prior knowledge establishes a framework for learning. When children recognize similarities between objects, ideas, or experiences, they are able to connect ideas and build on their knowledge base by adding to it or modifying concepts already in place. As educators encourage children to make meaningful associations with prior knowledge, conceptual understanding of ideas grows and learning is advanced. This particular approach to meaning making is useful in contemplating historical artifacts.

Introduction to Object Lesson

The object lesson begins with a small collection of keys. The objects in the collection are diverse and reflect typical, present-day keys juxtaposed with old-fashioned keys varying in size and shape, with individual keys reflecting different degrees of familiarity for preschoolers. The program introduction begins with the display of keys on a black, velvet cloth and leads to a discussion of the objects where children share their personal observations and thoughts. A few simple questions invite conversation. *What do you think about when you see these objects? What do you notice when you look closely? How are the objects the same and how are they different? How might these objects be used?*

Most of the children will likely recognize several of the objects as keys and will be able to explain the purpose of the objects in general terms, to open and close or lock and unlock something. The conversation should build on the knowledge that children already possess and then develop in complexity through a strategy of open-ended questioning, a technique widely used by history museums. Each tour or program will differ based upon the unique perspectives and background knowledge of the children and individual developmental levels.

Through a process of questioning and guided conversation, it becomes clear that all of the objects are keys and that they possess a variety of purposes that includes keeping personal property safe through the use of a lock. *What would you want to keep safe? Are there special objects in your home that your family would like to keep safe? What would happen if there weren't any keys? How would you solve that problem?*

This is a perfect time to share the idea that locks and keys are not new, but have been part of our world for centuries and that today's keys often look very different from other keys. This is an opportunity to make a connection to people of the past by inviting children to think not only about how these objects were used, but also about the people who used them. With this in mind, it is time to focus the children's attention on the historic keys. Invite the children to compare the physical attributes of the keys on display and listen

Object Lessons inspired by History Museums 87

carefully to their observations. Some children may note that they have seen the *unfamiliar keys* in cartoons, books, or other media forms.

Unlocking Mysteries of the Past

In this special program, preschoolers and families with little ones will become museum detectives tasked with identifying objects that require a special key. Frame this special role by saying that detectives will help us unlock the mysteries of the past by looking carefully, but also explain that the detectives have other responsibilities such as keeping everything safe by not touching. The focus is on careful looking while walking through the Mansion to find furniture, artifacts, and even parts of the building that could be opened or locked with a key. *How will you know if a special object or place might have a key?*

The evidence of a lock is the keyhole, at least in relationship to keys, but there are other types of locks such as bars on a door that children might mention. As children notice keyholes in drawers, cabinets, doors, and other historic objects, let them look at the collection of keys used in the introductory activity to ponder which key might fit the lock. Remind children that they will need to use their imagination as detectives since they won't be able to place keys in any of the locks. Model appropriate gestures for unlocking something and the children will eagerly join in the pretend play.

Young children will likely identify large keys for larger keyholes and smaller keys for the tiny ones. Selecting old-fashioned keys will also make sense to children since the objects in the house are old, thus suggesting that keys from the past will be the best choice. Children are literal in their interpretations and have good intuitive understanding of the world and how it works and will likely surprise many adults with their insights and questions.

Although many of the locks are found in predictable places like doors and cabinets, there will certainly be others that surprise or excite children. At Montpelier, much like other historic homes, there are unusual artifacts built for securing personal possessions, objects that are likely to be unfamiliar to children of the twenty-first century. The knife box is one such artifact, crafted of wood to hold the family silverware, some of the most expensive items in the home (Figure 7.1). Other storage containers such as tea caddies for storing tea leaves and sugar chests were constructed with locks to protect the precious cargo imported from overseas. Not only can these artifacts be found at Montpelier, but other artifacts with similar features are displayed throughout the historic home. Our young museum detectives may notice a wide variety of objects that require keys – blanket chests, sideboards for storing dishes, a small case known as a cellarette [to hold wine bottles], desks, china presses, and bookcases. Virtually everything was locked up to protect property from staff, paid or otherwise.

As artifacts are identified, engage the children in conversation through inquiry. *Where are the knives, forks, and spoons in your house? Is there a lock on the drawer? What about sugar, books, and blankets? Are they kept in locked*

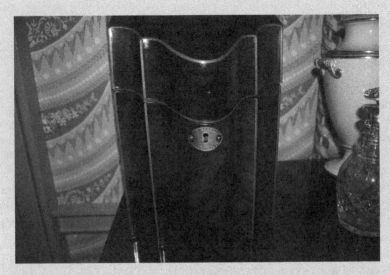

FIGURE 7.1 Knife box with lock from Montpelier Collection
Source: Courtesy of Montpelier, a National Trust Historic Site.

cabinets at your home? Throughout the Mansion there are many examples of objects that require keys. *Who do you think carried the keys?* According to Montpelier's Assistant Curator, Teresa Teixeira, there is a visitor account indicating that Dolley Madison held the keys (Interview, 2016). Throughout the tour of the Mansion, there will be evidence of keyed artifacts that children will notice, providing opportunities to continue the conversation. *Is this similar to what happens at home or is it different? What do you think?*

If children are curious about anomalies represented in life from the past, practices that are markedly different from today's practices, answer questions simply and directly. For example, children may wonder why it was necessary to have so many keys to lock everyday objects. The explanation should acknowledge that in James Madison's time, many wealthy families had slaves or servants working in their homes and there was fear that family treasures or possessions might be stolen by the slaves, the hired help, or anyone else visiting the home. Children will respond to this idea with thoughts of their own.

The heart of this experience is comparing life from the past with life today and connecting to people in history through objects. A simple key, as the foundation of the object lesson, offers a specific lens through which to view the past and then compare with today's world.

Lesson Conclusion

This object lesson opens conversation between children and adults, providing a purpose for looking carefully at the historic home and its many treasures. This everyday object, the key, serves as a catalyst for looking at artifacts of the past and understanding the life of people in the home. It's simple, yet effective as a strategy.

Since learning for the young child is active and primarily about process, ideally there would be locks and keys that children can use, whether in the introductory activity or integrated into some area of the historic home, possibly a children's hands-on space. For example, at Monticello, the home of Thomas Jefferson, there is a hands-on experience with locks in the Crossroads Exhibition.

> The exhibition's interactive components include a model of the wine dumbwaiter for visitors to operate, a "servant's" bell, and functional door locks, emphasizing the importance of locked storage spaces that led Jefferson's granddaughters to refer to housekeeping as "carrying the keys."
>
> *Monticello 2016*

An object lesson about keys makes the learning meaningful to preschoolers since they have a present-day reference point. Young children are curious about keys at a very early age and understand the purpose of the object from daily life scenarios as well as from listening to children's books. In one example, *Good Night, Gorilla* (Peggy Rathmann 2000), the zookeeper bids each animal goodnight and continues to stroll through the zoo, unaware that Gorilla has stolen his keys – large, old-fashioned skeleton keys, no less – to let every animal roam free for the evening. While listening to this bedtime story, a child sees images of keys and develops an understanding of context and purpose, valuable information for future reference.

As educators know, past experience contributes to a child's base knowledge and establishes a bridge between the old and the new. When young children visit an historic home, the key to success is making a meaningful connection between the familiar and the unfamiliar while also creating a unique role for the child that is engaging and purposeful. The idea of keys is one example, chosen from many possibilities, for engaging children through objects.

Object Lesson 2 History

The second object lesson emphasizes critical concepts in history, the idea of *past and present* as well as the concept of *change over time*. The essence of history is captured by those simple phrases. And through well-thought out experiences, the building blocks for understanding the idea of history is born and children begin a journey of connecting to the past. *In the Kitchen: Making Connections with Old-Fashioned Cooking Tools* creates a context for making the comparison between *then and now* as children examine kitchen tools from the early to mid-twentieth century and compare them with familiar items of today.

OBJECT LESSON: IN THE KITCHEN: MAKING CONNECTIONS WITH OLD-FASHIONED COOKING TOOLS

Bon Appetit! Julia Child's Kitchen at the Smithsonian – Legendary cook and teacher Julia Child (1912–2004) had a tremendous impact on food and culinary history in America. She inspired many Americans to conquer their fears of the unfamiliar and to expand their ideas about ingredients and flavors, tools and techniques, and meals in general.

Julia's kitchen from her Cambridge, Massachusetts, home provides both a starting point and a backdrop for this exhibition on changing foods and foodways in America in the second half of the 20th century. It contains tools and equipment from the late 1940s, when Julia Child began her life in food, through to 2001, when she donated this kitchen to the Smithsonian Institution.

National Museum of American History, Smithsonian Institution 2016

Background and Core Strategies

Young children are by their very nature visual learners who construct meaning by making visual comparisons, identifying similarities and differences to sort, order, and classify objects in their world. This ability to organize the physical environment, and eventually more abstract concepts, begins at a very early age as evidenced in informal play when toddlers and preschoolers sort blocks by color, arrange shells by shape, and order stuffed animals from largest to smallest. Museum educators can design educational programs to take advantage of this instinctive desire to make meaning through organization by encouraging children to look for similarities and differences when comparing artifacts in galleries and everyday objects from personal experience.

As children hone their observation skills through daily practice, they attend to detail and apply that information to real-world situations, making nuanced distinctions among toys in the playroom, dogs in the neighborhood, or different types of animals in books. This inclination to observe and compare is useful when introducing less familiar objects represented in history museums and becomes an effective strategy when comparing the known with the unknown.

Context for Object Lesson

In the twenty-first century, there are countless kitchen tools found in homes across America, from the garlic press and miniature grater to berry slicers and whisks of varying sizes. There seems to be a gadget for almost every task at hand. In homes where cooking is a priority and viewed with passion, children are exposed to different tools and techniques as they observe or participate in cooking experiences.

And while there are culinary connoisseurs in some homes, there are also many households where cooking and baking are less common and children rarely experience *made from scratch* foods for everyday meals, such as homemade breads or delicacies, such as cakes or cobbler. In the latter scenario, children are less likely to recognize simple cooking tools such as measuring spoons or spatulas. With the increase in restaurants located in virtually every community as well as the wide range of products offered in supermarkets, many families are choosing convenience over at-home cooking.

This knowledge is a reminder that children begin the journey of learning from different starting points. Effective educators quickly assess baseline knowledge of learners and adapt programs to accommodate the range of cognitive levels and needs of children.

Introduction to Object Lesson

Young children are passionate about pretend play and find joy in a simple wooden spoon and metal mixing bowl, a behavior observed by parents in most kitchens across the country. Ordinary kitchen tools like wooden spoons and metal bowls are objects recognized by most children and are terms that become integrated into common language in the early years.

A collection of simple, everyday objects used for cooking is the starting point for this object lesson. A large wooden spoon, a metal spatula, a set of colorful measuring spoons, a small mixing bowl, and a potato masher are objects that are most easily recognized by children. By adding a rolling pin, a grater, a lemon zester, and a nut cracker to the mix, the experience will challenge preschoolers to identify less-familiar objects while also increasing interest due to the infusion of novelty. It is important to remember that some children will have little experience even with the most common household items.

To begin the lesson, invite children to look closely at the array of kitchen tools and then use open-ended questions to spark conversation. *What do you think about when you see these objects? Where might you find them? How are they used? What questions do you have about the objects? How are they the same? How are they different?* Familiarity with a few objects will inspire conversation and the sharing of experiences. Novelty will create interest. Briefly model the use of several objects by using appropriate gestures or body language and explain that there are many different types of cooking tools with this being a very small collection.

Shift the conversation from familiar kitchen tools to the museum experience by asking children if they know what it means to be curious. As part of the discussion on curiosity, model a sense of wonder or curiosity by gestures and comments such as "I wonder what this might be." *Are you ever curious about anything?* Ignite children's curiosity with a special object, a Curiosity Box, a place for important objects. Again, model a sense of wonder and encourage children to think about what might be inside the box. Listen carefully to the wonderful ideas that children share. As paraphrased from Aristotle, "Learning begins in wonder" and encouraging a sense of wonder nurtures learning in the young.

In the Kitchen: Making Connections with Old-Fashioned Cooking Tools

An old-fashioned, wooden masher is a great tool to tuck away in the Curiosity Box and ideal for investigating with young museum visitors. Set the stage for the conversation with a few questions before the box is opened and the artifact revealed. *What can you tell us about the size of the object? What do you know about the weight of the object? Do you think that there is one object in the box or many? What makes you think that?* Introductory questions encourage children to think logically and make predictions based upon the information gathered through handling the Curiosity Box. *Is there any way for you to know the color of the object in the box?* Remind the children that we use our senses of sight, sound, taste, touch, and smell to gather information and that our understanding is limited in some cases. In this particular case, it is impossible to be certain of the color of an object in the Curiosity Box, but we can know if the object is heavy or light by holding the box.

After the initial discussion, open the box and remove the artifact (an old-fashioned masher). Hold the masher with care and demonstrate respect for the object when touching. Encourage the children to look carefully at the artifact and then think of one word that describes the teaching object. Words will vary from child to child – heavy, brown, wooden, rough – with some words more sophisticated than others based on each child's experience. Expect some children to repeat a word offered by a previous child, a common occurrence with young learners. A perfect response to the repetition of ideas is to acknowledge how interesting it is that several children noticed the same thing about the artifact. The conversation is also enriched when children are asked to explain their thinking behind their descriptive word. *What made you say that the object is rough? Which of your senses tells you this?* In this way, children are able to learn from one another.

The conversation will naturally evolve with queries from the children as well as educator-based questions. *How do you think this object might have been used?* It might be necessary to provide a clue to guide the inquiry, possibly the room where the object is used, in this case, the kitchen or cooking area. Preschoolers often have a strong intuitive understanding based on prior knowledge, which drives the discussion toward possible uses for the tool. In all likelihood, at least one child will suggest that the object is a tool used in cooking, possibly to mash, smash, or grind food. Validate ideas presented and confirm the purpose of the old-fashioned masher. However, it also makes sense to let children know that it is not uncommon for people to use the same tool in different ways. The ability of such young learners to make meaning about the unknown may come as a surprise to some, but the experienced early childhood educator understands the sophistication of preschoolers and their capacity to make sense of the world.

The gallery activity begins with a few simple questions to guide children's thinking. *Do all mashers look alike? What do you think?* Invite the group to look carefully at the cooking tools in Julia Child's kitchen to see which ones might be appropriate for mashing apples, potatoes, or other foods. Encourage the children to think about how Julia's tools compare with the masher from the Curiosity Box.

After the gallery experience, restate the opening questions. *Do all mashers look alike? How do you know?* Stress the importance of grounding thinking in the evidence found in the gallery. At this point, it makes sense to reintroduce the initial set of cooking tools, possibly adding a few others that are similar in function to the old-fashioned masher, to extend the conversation based on the children's interest.

A key concept grounding this object lesson is that tools are important in everyone's life, now and in the past, but that the design of tools and their purpose change with new thinking and materials. This is true of cooking tools, building tools, or any other type of tools. The idea that many of today's cooking tools are different from kitchen tools of the past becomes clear through this gallery experience. It also encourages a new discussion about the future and the types of tools that will be created.

Lesson Conclusion

Julia Child's Kitchen at the Smithsonian is an exhibition that has appeal for young and old alike. For preschoolers and families interested in spending more time in the exhibit, suggest a search for interesting tools that might be compared with other more familiar gadgets. Suggest that children look carefully at other types of kitchen tools used by Julia and share their ideas about the use of each gadget.

Another activity focuses on tools of the future. Plan an activity where children will design kitchen tools for the future, either by drawing special tools or constructing gadgets using art materials or found objects. Allow for time to share ideas and encourage children to explain why their new tool will be helpful for work in the kitchen. Recognize children's efforts and innovative thinking. The joy of this gallery-based object lesson is the simple connection between objects of today and artifacts of the past by using a hands-on approach for engaging young children.

Object Lesson 3 History

The third object lesson is inspired by an outdoor, living history museum where the past is brought to life through unique interpretive strategies. This type of museum captures the spirit of a particular time or place and offers an immersive experience that allows visitors to be part of the story. It is a particularly apt environment for children to make sense of their world since they are naturally drawn to exploration of ideas through narrative enhanced by imagination.

> **OBJECT LESSON: THE TRAVELER'S TRUNK**
>
> Old Sturbridge Village, the largest outdoor history museum in the Northeast, depicts a rural New England town of the 1830s. Founded in 1946, the Village has 60 original buildings across 200 acres; each carefully researched, restored, and brought to the museum site from towns throughout New England. These include homes, meetinghouses, a district school, country store, bank, law office, print shop, carding mill, gristmill, pottery, blacksmith shop, shoe shop, cooper shop, and an accurately reproduced sawmill.
>
> Old Sturbridge Village 2016
>
> **Background and Core Strategies**
>
> Research tells us that children understand their world through storytelling and narrative. According to John Falk and Lynn Dierking (2000), "Children as young as three years seem to remember familiar daily experiences in terms of scripts or stories, organized representations of event sequences that provide a general description of what occurs and when it occurs in a given situation" (p. 48). Story is often the vehicle for communicating particular ideas, concepts, or even cultural understanding. In families, individuals "build knowledge and understanding through conversation" which leads to shared meanings (ibid., p. 38). Not only do children learn about their world through stories, but they interpret their world and express personal ideas, values, and feelings in a narrative format.
>
> Imaginative play is yet another important aspect of every young child's world and serves as a means of making meaning and considering the possibilities of the real world. Imaginative play often revolves around the unique perspective of a young child and adopts a creative view of the world. This is evident in a child's experimentation with an empty box and the use of that box in various play scenarios, first, as a boat, next as a robot, and finally as a spaceship. Imaginative play empowers children to re-enact roles encountered through personal experience and fills in the gaps where there is lack of information or insight. Through imaginative play, children act on their perceptions of the world and develop greater awareness through their social interactions with peers. These two strategies, storytelling and imaginative play, are easily applied to museum programs and together will serve as a viable tool for engaging young learners with history.

Introduction to Object Lesson

Story becomes the defining feature for the introduction to this object lesson. Read Leslie Connor's (2004) *Miss Bridie Chose a Shovel*, a delightful children's book about the journey of an immigrant coming to America in the mid-nineteenth century. Children will explore the concept of immigration in a broad sense as they learn about Miss Bridie's journey and also discover from the story that prudence is important for those venturing to a new country. The story of Miss Bridie's shovel encourages children to reflect on their own choices in life and imagine what it would be like to step into the shoes of someone from the past.

America's history is a story of immigrants and how they journeyed from afar. Connor's story will introduce preschoolers to the idea of immigrants coming to America and encourage them to think about objects they would choose to bring on a journey to a new land. As children share their thoughts about Miss Bridie's choice of a shovel, there is an opportunity to challenge them to explain their own preferences under similar circumstances.

The Traveler's Trunk

Old Sturbridge Village represents the arrival of immigrants to America and their life in rural New England in the 1830s. Like Miss Bridie, the inhabitants of New England villages reflected in Old Sturbridge Village brought along carefully selected objects on their journey to America. Trunks, frequently packed with belongings for the long journey, are interesting artifacts that will spark the imagination of children as they think about treasures brought to America by immigrants. Begin a conversation by looking at one trunk and describe the owner. Invite the children to imagine the objects carried in the trunk and think about how they were used in the village. The creativity of children will provide a vast array of suggestions about objects packed in the trunk.

The second activity begins with a document listing the contents of a trunk. Talk about the collection of items in the trunk and ask the children to speculate about the owner. *What do the objects in the trunk tell us about the owner? Does this trunk belong to a man or a woman? What is the profession or type of work of the owner? Which of the objects do you think were most important to the person? What else can you tell about the owner from his or her belongings?* Complete the discussion with an imaginative story, created by the children and based upon the objects in the trunk.

A third activity begins with storytelling about Old Sturbridge Village and some of the early members of the community from the country store clerk to the printer, followed by imaginative play using costumes and props. After the storytelling, invite the children to create stories and portray individuals from the village. A reproduction of a trunk from the Old Sturbridge Village collection, filled with facsimiles of costumes from the mid-1800s, sets the stage for the children to recreate stories and reimagine the lives of immigrants from a time long ago.

Lesson Conclusion

Living history museums like Old Sturbridge Village are exciting entry points into the past and provide children with a real-world, immersive experience that engages the imagination. Although there are myriad opportunities for exploration during visits to these special environments, children and families will build memories around encounters that are rich in sensory experience, stimulating the mind and imagination. Find new opportunities to imagine the stories of immigrants coming to American and share ideas about what they brought with them on their journeys. Return to the initial conversation about Miss Bridie's shovel and ask the children to talk about packing a bag for a long journey to a new land. And take advantage of conversations with costumed interpreters who invite visitors, young and old, to step into the past. For a young child, this immersive experience could be the start of a love affair with history.

Conclusion

History is often thought of as a subject reserved for older students and less often a topic conceived of as appropriate for younger children. Yet when preschoolers are exposed to content related to the past, they gain knowledge about people, places, and events even without having a sophisticated understanding of chronology and other aspects related to time. As children mature and develop numerical understanding, their experiences reflecting the past begin to fill in the timeline that we associate with history.

Encounters with historical artifacts, photographs, and immersive environments are a wonderful opportunity for children to connect to history and the stories of people from the past. It is never too early to introduce children to history as long as it's clear that preschoolers and kindergartners make sense of artifacts in a way that differs from adults. Their understanding will come from story or will relate to connections with prior knowledge based on personal experience. For young children, thoughtful programs and experiences will build historical thinking, connect children to people and events from the past, and support the growth of cognitive skills. With children's natural curiosity and desire to explore, history museums offer unique opportunities for learning and making meaning about the world.

8

OBJECT LESSONS INSPIRED BY ART MUSEUMS, SCULPTURE GARDENS, AND PUBLIC ART

> Our task, regarding creativity, is to help children climb their own mountains, as high as possible. No one can do more.
>
> Loris Malaguzzi, in Edwards et al. (2012), p. 52

Introduction

In the not so distant past, preschoolers were an anomaly in the art gallery. The rare presence of a young child among paintings and sculpture was likely in the context of a family visit, but in most cases with little acknowledgment that the museum could be a place of learning for little ones. In today's art museum, at least in the majority of western cultures, this is no longer the case as witnessed by the broad interest within the field driven by the excitement expressed by parents and local communities. This growing attention is certainly not exclusive to art museums, but is evident across all types of museums.

This growth comes at a time when there is increased interest in nurturing creativity in young children, and the art gallery, as an icon of ingenuity and imagination, is finding its role in advancing this goal. In both art museums and schools, creativity is a hallmark of excellence and is an underlying tenet of highly acclaimed programs. This passion for creativity is noted in the words of Loris Malaguzzi, the visionary founder of the Reggio Emilia early childhood model, when he stresses the value of helping "children climb their own mountains" as they learn to express their thoughts and ideas, often through a range of art materials. Malaguzzi understood that art was essential to children's lives.

With the support of increased funding from foundations and other organizations, the twenty-first-century art museum is now crafting engaging programs for the young, making galleries a place where preschoolers and kindergartners are invited to look, reflect, and connect with works of art. The newest trend supported by research examines possible benefits for introducing art to babies and toddlers. This shift aligns with the changing attitude of educators and other museum professionals toward the capacity of young children to explore and engage in meaningful ways with works of art. It is an opportunity to connect children with their own creativity.

Art Museums, Sculpture Gardens, and Public Art

There are amazing ways to acquaint young children with the aesthetic world given the wide-ranging diversity among art institutions and public spaces showcasing grand works of art. It is also important for children to know that art is not represented in museums alone, but is woven throughout the everyday world. Opportunities are becoming a reality in many museums with more and more preschoolers, toddlers, and even babies enjoying art through programs designed by educators based upon current research and pioneering efforts within the field (Danko-McGhee 2013). The object lessons inspired by art museums, sculpture gardens, and public art described in this chapter merely touch the surface of what can be imagined.

Object Lesson 1 Art

OBJECT LESSON: EXPERIENCING ART THROUGH PLAY: EXPLORING TOPS

Art: Los Trompos ("Spinning Tops") at the High Museum of Art (April 24–November 1, 2015).

Los Trompos ("Spinning Tops") is the High's second large-scale, interactive design installation by contemporary Mexican designers Héctor Esrawe and Ignacio Cadena on the Woodruff Arts Center's Carroll Slater Sifly Piazza. This site-specific work continues a multi-year initiative to activate the outdoor space and engage visitors. As a blank canvas for community engagement and programming, Los Trompos draws its inspiration from the form of a spinning top, a toy popular with children around the world. The project features over 30 three-dimensional, larger-than-life tops in a variety of colors and shapes installed throughout the Piazza. The colorful surfaces of each "top" will be created in part by flat nylon rope woven in a traditional Mexican style. By working together, visitors will be able to spin the tops on their bases as they interact with the structures.

High Museum of Art 2015

Background and Core Strategies

Play is a unique platform for learning and recognized by educators and theorists as a significant factor in a child's development. In the words of Russian-born theorist, Lev Vygotsky, play and learning are synonymous. Play "contains all developmental tendencies in a condensed form and is itself a major source of development" (Vygotsky 1978, p. 102). The benefits of play and its role in museum programming are a relatively new phenomenon for museum professionals, but a strategy that is growing not only in practice but also gaining respect.

Children make sense of their world through play, pretending to be a pirate while watching *Peter Pan* or stirring imaginary cake batter while observing a parent baking desserts for a festive holiday party. In play, children find opportunities to explore and imagine when they encounter an unknown object at the park or examine a newly designed box of cereal at the grocery store. Objects are reimagined to become part of a child's pretend world.

There are many opportunities to engage young children with art by thinking about possible connections to a child's everyday life. Consider Los Trompos (Spinning Tops) and some of those unique opportunities. A practical introduction begins with play and toy tops. Children experiment with wooden tops, observing each toy closely as it spins and then slowly tilts to the side as the momentum shifts from fast to slow. Through trial and error, children learn that there is a specific technique of positioning the top to keep it upright and spinning; with careful observation, children recognize patterns of movement associated with tops and make discoveries based on what is visible in play. At this stage, understanding is often intuitive and can be acted upon more readily than expressed through language. Children's natural inclination to explore and imagine leads to insight into how things work which becomes background knowledge for future encounters. Play is a unique platform for learning.

Introduction to Lesson

The object lesson is defined by a collection of child-friendly tops, perfect for play and recognized by many children the world over. In children's play, toy tops become a source of information and also an entry point for thinking about the art object.

Cognitive developmental theory recognizes play as instrumental in a child's learning. Children need time and space for unstructured play to observe and experiment with materials. They also benefit from experiences that allow them to fully engage in play and direct their own experience, thereby, increasing motivation and opportunity for learning. Time for play in the early minutes of a program increases the likelihood that meaningful connections will be made to an artwork with a common theme, so remember to allow for exploratory play in the opening moments of this lesson.

A few simple questions from a parent, a museum educator, or a classroom teacher complement the play and encourage the children to think about what they see. *How did you get the top to spin? What technique did you use? What happens if you tilt your top to one side when you start spinning? Can you describe what happens to the colors on the top while it's spinning? What changes can you see? What do you think is most interesting about your top?* This interaction should be spontaneous, rather than an adult-directed activity. Similar questions will become important as the children experience the art work on the Piazza.

Experiencing the Art

A simple question or two offers a transition from the wooden tops to the art installation of Los Trompos (Figure 8.1). *If an artist loves the idea of spinning tops, what would his art work look like? What would the artist create?* Invite the children to share ideas and encourage creative thinking, letting the children know that each artist will imagine spinning tops in a different way. This is a perfect moment to have a brief conversation about artists, particularly with preschoolers who likely have limited experience with museums or art. A simple exchange introduces the idea of imagination and how each person has ideas that can be expressed in different ways, in words, through paintings or sculpture, or in performance (dance, music, and theater). Children are fully aware of the term imagination and will readily share personal experiences that relate to imaginative thinking.

The initial sighting of Los Trompos will be a magical experience, whether walking onto the Piazza by the High Museum of Art in Atlanta or seeing the

FIGURE 8.1 Children enjoy the interactive installation "Los Trompos" ("The Spinning Tops") on the High Museum of Art's Carroll Slater Sifly Piazza. Created by Mexican designers Héctor Esrawe and Ignacio Cadena, the site-specific installation was commissioned by the High as part of its multi-year initiative to activate the Museum's outdoor space.

Source: Photo by Abel Klainbaum.

installation in some other place, so be prepared for the look of surprise on children's faces and the excitement they express when sharing their feelings and ideas about the installation. *Is this what you expected to see? What words would you use to describe the art? What do you think it might feel like to spin inside one of these tops? How are these spinners the same as your wooden tops? How are they different? What do you like about this art?* In all likelihood, the magnitude of the art, as well as the intense and varied colors, will capture everyone's attention. Allow children to fully engage and experience the art installation, and then interact with children naturally by asking open-ended questions that encourage a personal response. Informally, children will be able to share observations about size, shape, color, or some other attribute associated with what they see. Invite more complex thinking such as comparing several of the artist's tops. Although comparisons require more critical observation and higher-order thinking, most young children have the capacity to recognize similarities and differences.

A unique characteristic of this art installation is the open invitation to step into the artwork and experience it by spinning like a top. For every visitor this is memorable, but for most children the experience is euphoric! There is a sense of freedom in the exploration of the art. And while the interaction with the installation will immerse the children fully, the experience can be enriched with a simple conversation that focuses on the artist's choices of materials, colors, and construction. It is the perfect moment to let children observe changes in color or even the shape of the spinners when moving. *Did the colors on the artist's spinning tops change in the same way as the colors on your toy top?*

Further Investigation and Concluding Activity

A culminating activity for this object lesson introduces yet another way of thinking about the installation and can make connections to the tactile nature of the art. There are many possibilities for rich, hands-on experiences that range from art-making emphasizing color or materials to continued exploration of movement. One idea allows children to experiment with strips of colorful fabric, pieces of cord, or even varied shades of yarn to create their own works of art by carefully wrapping the material around a frame. Another option invites children to creatively imagine and design a colorful top using a technique of collage with different cutout shapes. A performance-based activity can encourage children to twirl like a top while listening to music, twirling slowly, then faster, on tip-toes, or close to the ground like an ice skater spinning. By describing different types of movement children are challenged to connect words to movements. This is a time to remind children that it is important to listen carefully to directions so that no one gets overly dizzy. Safety is important. While a few children perform, the rest of the group can critique their creative movements; then have a new group perform. Add colored scarves to

> performances to enhance the visual experience of the movement. Any of these activities will expand thinking beyond the initial experience of tops and can lead to conversation about artist techniques or movement of objects.
>
> Children's impressions from a morning with Los Trompos will certainly become lasting memories. *What will you remember about this art? What do you know now that you didn't know before? Did you know that it is possible to step into art?* A final look at the artist's magnificent tops will reinforce memory. Ask the children to snap a picture using a pretend camera and save the picture for later recall. This interactive experience with *Los Trompos* will be remembered for many years to come.

Los Trompos was second in a series of large-scale works commissioned for the Museum's piazza and conceived to explore how engagement with art and design can extend beyond the museum's walls. Replacing what had previously been an expansive concrete space with 32 brightly colored, life-sized spinning tops, was thrilling! For many children, Los Trompos was a huge playground. They ran from top to top, spinning and taking rides in each of the four different designs. For some children, the tops with protected interiors provided an intimate space to have lunch with a friend or to quietly read a book with a parent. Los Trompos inspired many art-making opportunities for our family audience. Families took part in weaving workshops, created whimsical spinning sculptures on the piazza, and made paintings that attempted to capture the circular movement of the installation.

Nicole Cromartie, Educator, Manager of Family Programs, High Museum of Art 2015

Object Lesson 2 Art

The second object lesson explores narrative in art through the lens of everyday life and at the same time contributes to a child's understanding of a critical concept in history, change over time. Édouard Manet's 1875 painting, *Laundry*, represents a common task embedded in family life – the idea of washing clothing, a depiction that contrasts for many children with their twenty-first-century personal experience, at least those living in many western cultures. The narrative portrayed in the painting holds meaning for children even with its historical context and offers several different reference points for most preschoolers. The opportunity to interpret stories in paintings, particularly those with some familiar ties, is an invitation for children to share personal narratives and make sense of their own world.

> **OBJECT LESSON: EVERYDAY LIFE IN ART: WASHBOARDS AND CLOTHES PINS**
>
> Art: *Laundry* (*Le Linge*) by Édouard Manet at the Barnes Foundation, Philadelphia.

Manet's 1875 Impressionist painting depicts everyday life of a mother and child engaged in washing family clothes. A young child looks closely at a wooden wash tub and also observes her mother wringing water from an article of clothing. In the background, wash is hanging on a line to dry.

Background and Core Strategies

Young children learn through narrative and storytelling. This entry point for learning is defined by researchers John Falk and Lynn Dierking (2000) as a socio-cultural sharing of information. Their research, as noted earlier, recognizes the significance of narrative in the lives of young children as a strategy for expressing ideas and capturing memories, and further advances the belief that "scripts are the basic building blocks for people's structured knowledge, a basic means through which they organize, interpret, and predict their world" (ibid., p. 48).

As research indicates, children are drawn to stories at an early age, acquiring information in a story format through social encounters as well as through the world of children's literature. Children's experiences with narrative are vast, and range from the simple, everyday descriptions of events embedded in social interactions to lively tales recounted by mothers and fathers, aunts and uncles, grandparents and friends about cultural traditions and family history. In their early years, children learn that life is made up of stories and that the story is a means of expressing personal thoughts and ideas. This knowledge guides children as they express their own ideas and interact with others. A story captures a child's attention and gives meaning to ideas through appropriate context while also increasing a child's interest. Narrative becomes the foundation for understanding and communicating ideas.

Children also discover that stories are conveyed not only through words, although this is the most familiar or common approach, but also by gestures and movement as well as visually through images. Through performance and art, children enter the world of interpretation and learn to translate actions and images into words that express a point of view.

Introduction to the Lesson

The subject of Manet's painting, *Laundry*, offers some interesting possibilities for exploration. The object lesson's initial activity aims to introduce children to ideas related to the painting's theme and serves as preparation for looking closely and responding to the work of art. It is a time to focus attention and increase interest using a small teaching collection of objects. Several options are suggested.

For the novice visitor to the art museum, begin with a collection of objects visible in Manet's painting – cotton clothes line rope, a sunflower, a wooden wash bucket, an article of clothing similar to one in the painting. Invite the children to look closely at the painting, then at the objects in the teaching collection, and describe where in the painting they see the objects. This is a very literal experience, but appropriate for first-time preschool or kindergarten visitors.

A more sophisticated lesson highlights a few clothes pins and later introduces an old-fashioned washboard: novel objects that intrigue most young children, thereby sparking curiosity. So while there is novelty, it is likely that children have a reference point for interpreting these objects either through play or from preschool experiences where clothes pins are present in the art center, carefully holding paper to easels. Children may also be familiar with clothes pins from children's stories such as *Three Little Kittens* (Galdone 1986) where they appear in the context of hanging mittens up to dry. The aim of this experience is to encourage children to make observations and interpret what is happening in the painting, then consider other objects that are relevant to the painting, even though they may not be visible. The exercise encourages children to think critically.

Begin the lesson by displaying a collection of clothes pins, preferably different types, and ask children to examine the objects using their senses. *What do you think about when you see these objects? Did you discover anything interesting when you looked more closely or touched one of the clothes pins? What else do you know about these objects? Can you think of different ways that clothes pins can be used?* Although prior knowledge for most children will not necessarily include laundering as it's depicted in the painting, it is very likely that at least one child, if not several, will associate clothes pins with hanging clothes on a washline and will contribute that information to the conversation to enrich the learning of others. This sharing of ideas with peers exemplifies Vygotsky's notion of socially mediated learning.

Children's exploration and conversation about clothespins will set the stage for looking at Manet's painting. For educators, it is helpful to note that the experience will be most effective if informal and conversational, allowing children to drive the process.

Experiencing the Art

The art experience begins with careful looking. It is exciting to anticipate the children's initial reaction to *Laundry* since it is a rather large canvas with vivid colors. A natural response to the art may open a conversation before the educator asks a single question. Follow the lead of the children and at some point focus their attention on the subject of the painting. *What do you notice first when you look at this painting? Did you know that the artist is telling a story in this painting? What clues does he give us about the story? Think about our collection of clothes pins. Even though we may not see them in the painting, can you imagine how they connect to the story the artist is telling? What do you think?*

The narrative expressed in *Laundry* becomes clear to children as they notice the mother and child, the tub, and clothes hanging on a line. The woman's actions, wringing water from cloth, is a starting point for telling a story. *What do you think is happening in this picture? Who is doing the work? Imagine that this is a page in a book. What do you think happened just before this picture? If we turn the page, what do you think will happen next? Let's tell the whole story, not just the part that we see in the painting.*

As children share ideas to develop the story, there is an opportunity to introduce an old-fashioned washboard to expand notions of laundering clothing by hand. Encourage children to ask questions; provide ideas about the artifact, explaining the purpose of a washboard if necessary and demonstrating its use. After further exploration and discussion, create an imaginative game where children pretend to scrub clothes on the washboard and hang them on an imaginary line. It could be a retelling of *Three Little Kittens* or another tale. Preschoolers will eagerly engage in pretend play.

Concluding Activity

Once children become co-creators of the story that complements Manet's painting, they will be primed to tell personal stories about washing clothes. Stories will vary from child to child; some will reflect reality while others are situated in the realm of imagination. As children are enjoying their own storytelling, suggest that they have a conversation with their grandparents or great grandparents. *How did your family wash clothes when they were little? Is a washboard a familiar object for grandparents and great-grandparents?* Cross-generational stories are a gift to young and old alike, and will likely become life-long, treasured memories.

According to a museum educator at the Barnes Foundation:

> *The Laundry*, a work of art by Édouard Manet, offers young children a chance to explore narrative in art in classrooms and galleries at the Barnes Foundation. Children find a natural connection to the work of art and through close looking and thoughtful reflection, think about their personal stories.
>
> A favorite activity connected to this lesson is bubble painting. The children discuss objects needed to wash clothes and then mix these materials – soap and water – with paint to create a fun, soapy mixture that produces colorful bubbles. The preschoolers then use straws to blow bubbles that pop when covered with a piece of white paper leaving behind colorful bubble shaped outlines. The sensory exploration of bubble painting, coupled with the gallery experience of looking at Manet's work of art, creates long-lasting memories for the children.

Object Lesson 3 Art

The third object lesson connects children to the idea of art-making with familiar objects. These *found objects* are easily recognized as part of the everyday world, yet are unexpected elements in museum artworks. It is exciting for children to experience art that is familiar and at the same time unique in its creation. A Calder mobile in the National Gallery of Art, Washington, DC, made of wire, sea glass, and a simple key is easily recognized as a fish, but has added interest for a child due to its unique composition and materials that become the scales of the sea creature. At the Smithsonian's American Art Museum, a giraffe made from bottle caps is familiar and yet at the same time unique where metal caps from bottles equate with the spots of the animal. For young children, art takes on new meaning with the discovery of new possibilities for what art can be and how it can be created. It opens the door for a child's imagination and excitement for creating.

OBJECT LESSON: MAGICAL IDEAS: FOUND OBJECTS IN ART

Art: *Untitled (Aviary with Yellow Birds)* at the Hirshhorn Museum and Sculpture Garden.

Artist: Joseph Cornell, American

Medium: Wood, cork, paint, and cardboard in glass-fronted wood box; Date: c. 1948.

Exhibition History: HIRSHHORN MUSEUM AND SCULPTURE GARDEN, Smithsonian Institution, Washington, DC. "At the Hub of Things: New Views of the Collection," 16 October 2014–24 April 2016, no catalog.

Background and Core Strategies

Children enter this world curious and with a vivid imagination. A child's ability to imagine allows for making meaning about what is experienced. Einstein (1929) recognized the value of this ability, saying, "Imagination is more important than knowledge. For knowledge is limited, whereas imagination embraces the entire world, stimulating progress, giving birth to evolution." Merriam-Webster's definition of imagination, "the act or power of forming a mental image of something not present to the senses or never before wholly perceived in reality" (Merriam-Webster Dictionary 2015), offers insight into why Einstein's perspective might be true. Imagination opens the door for thinking about something new or unknown to recognize the possibilities of what might be. As children imagine possibilities, they experiment with ideas, make discoveries, and construct meaning about their world. Imaginative thinking takes a child beyond his limited experience. The ability to imagine represents higher-order thinking and is essential in problem-solving.

Joseph Cornell's art assemblages, also known as shadow boxes, evoke memories connected to the everyday objects arranged in the art work. These memory or dream boxes often symbolize sophisticated concepts, but also allow for personal interpretation by museum visitors. Young children will likely recognize basic themes or ideas in an individual shadow box, drawing from their knowledge of the everyday objects that make up the art work. They also will be intrigued by the small objects contained in each shadow box and imagine stories reflecting the collection. Cornell's assemblages are a wonderful inspiration for children's own creative endeavors with *found objects*.

Introduction to the Lesson

Victorian bric-a-brac, corks from wine bottles, natural materials from leaves and pine cones to broken branches, old photographs, pictures from books or magazines, buttons and bottle caps, textile scraps, plastic lids and spoons, and other inexpensive trinkets are typical of objects that appear in Cornell's shadow boxes and the art work of other artists who create with simple, well-known objects. A collection of everyday objects, also described as *found objects*, offers young children a tangible entry point for thinking about Cornell's art work. The choice of objects making up the collection for this lesson will be different for each museum educator.

Set the stage for open discussion. Display the collection of *found objects* on a black cloth and invite the children to talk about the objects. *What do you see? What can you tell us about the objects? Are there any objects that are unfamiliar? Can you imagine what each might be?* Select four or five objects from the collection and invite the children to think about what the objects have in common. Ask them to tell a story that would connect all the objects. Illustrate the activity using four or five objects from the collection that represent nature – a pine cone, a leaf, a branch, a flower. *How are these objects the same?* Another theme might be a birthday celebration – a photograph of cupcakes, a plastic spoon, birthday candles, a small piece of gift wrap, and ribbon. *What do you think about when you look at this group of objects?* In lieu of wooden boxes, place related objects in a cardboard mat frame that mirrors a shadow box. End the activity by saying that some artists collect everyday or *found objects* for art making and that Joseph Cornell is one of those special artists. Read *Mr. Cornell's Dream Boxes* (Jeanette Winter 2014) before entering the gallery to look at *Untitled: Aviary with Yellow Birds*.

Experiencing the Art

Introduce the gallery experience by inviting the children to be museum detectives. *Let's look for a work of art by Joseph Cornell. Is there anything special about his work that you remember?* Encourage the children to think about the boxes and also the objects that were so important to Cornell and his art. To guide looking toward a specific piece by Cornell, show the children a small nest, as a provocation. *This object is a clue for finding a specific art work created by Joseph Cornell. What does the nest tell us?*

With these clues, the children will likely identify *Untitled: Aviary with Yellow Birds* with little assistance. Once the shadow box is identified, encourage the children to look closely at the objects in the box. Invite the children to share personal observations and encourage them to think about the artist's role in creating the art work. *What objects would you add to this art work?* Remind the children about *Mr. Cornell's Dream Boxes* and ask them what he might have been dreaming about before making this shadow box.

Conclude the gallery experience by looking at other Cornell shadow boxes, or if none are on display, show photographs of his work so that the children see the variety of dream boxes and their themes.

Concluding Activity

Provide a wide array of everyday objects for art-making and remind the children that they are artists. Encourage everyone to look carefully at the objects and then choose four or five objects from the collection to create their own dream box. Provide cardboard mats, as modeled earlier in the lesson, to serve as shadow boxes. This activity will work best if there are multiple tables with objects, each table facilitated by an adult. Divide children into small groups for work at one table as a way to allow for adult guidance.

It will be important to encourage children to think about their choices of objects. *Tell me what your objects have in common. What is the story of your dream box?* Remind the children of the examples from earlier in the lesson, the nature-themed objects and the birthday celebration. Encourage them to use their imagination.

As children complete their dream boxes, create a miniature exhibition. Remind the children that Joseph Cornell's shadow boxes were displayed for the children just as their dream boxes are on display for others to see.

Object Lesson 4 Art

The fourth lesson explores kinetic sculpture and encourages children to think about the possibilities for movement in art, a concept that is novel for most preschoolers who likely perceive art in the context of their own experiences of painting and drawing. And while many children have experienced art-making that goes beyond the two-dimensional expression of painting and drawing to include three-dimensional sculpture, the range of artistic endeavors experienced by young children exists in a world where movement in art is not the norm. This lesson challenges children's preconceived ideas and opens the door for an experience that creates excitement and new discoveries.

OBJECT LESSON: MOVEMENT IN ART

Art: *Cluster of Four Cubes* by George Rickey at the National Gallery of Art Sculpture Garden.

George Rickey began to produce kinetic sculpture in the late 1940s. Intrigued by both the history of constructivist art and by the example of Calder's mobiles, he developed systems of motion that made his works respond to the slightest variations in the flow of air currents. Rickey's kinetic sculpture provides a dialogue between ordered geometric shapes and random motion.

The massive element of *Cluster of Four Cubes* is suspended by ball bearings to slender arms that branch from a central post. Each cube is precisely weighted and balanced, engineered to turn effortlessly in the lightest breeze; they glide, nearly brushing one another in an intricate and graceful dance that belies their apparent bulk.

National Gallery of Art 2016

Background and Core Strategies

Movement is essential to a young child's life. It is a predictable behavior associated with a child's natural inclination to explore and experience his world. Through movement, children are empowered to interact with their environment and build knowledge using all of their senses. Both movement and sensory experiences are exploratory strategies evident in play, an activity defined as a child's most important work (Piaget 1951). In the twenty-first century, experience, play, and movement are integrally woven into a young child's approach to learning, mirroring constructivist theory (Dewey [1938] 1963; Bruner 1960; Vygotsky 1966).

A child's natural affinity for movement easily extends beyond his physical interaction with the environment to include recognition that movement is also part of his world. This is evident in a young child's fascination with inanimate objects that move, such as ceiling fans that spin endlessly or whirling tops for children's play, as in the first object lesson. If it moves, a very young child pays attention.

Children are attracted to movement in most situations, whether inanimate objects or living creatures. A kitten playing with a ball of yarn attracts a young child's attention more readily than a sleeping kitty resting next to that same fuzzy ball. Movement brings novelty and the unexpected, characteristics that increase interest and motivation to learn.

Introduction to Lesson

Through experience, preschoolers intuitively understand that some things move naturally while others are more likely to remain at rest. This introductory lesson explores that concept. Place a collection of wooden blocks of different shapes – rectangular prisms, cubes, and cylinders – on a black cloth and ask children to describe the objects. *What do you know about these objects?* Encourage everyone to talk about their experiences with blocks and building. Extend the conversation by asking if a block can move and, if so, how can it move? Most children will realize that blocks do not move independently, but rather rely on someone or something to move them.

Continue the introductory lesson with a few simple questions. *What is movement? Can you show everyone what it means to move?* Every child will want to participate in this activity and will enthusiastically demonstrate movement using their bodies. Ask them to think of one way to move and then demonstrate that movement by working in small groups of two or three, continuing until everyone has a turn. Encourage the children to observe their friends' actions, focusing their attention on specific types of movement by acknowledging large movements, small movements, and unique approaches that children incorporate into their demonstrations. Remind everyone that some things move independently while others do not and suggest that it is sometimes surprising to discover that some things move that we don't expect.

Experiencing the Art

Before looking at the sculpture, remind the children about the idea of movement and its connection to the art by using a question to focus attention. *Do you think that art moves? What about a painting ... a decorative pot ... a sculpture?* Let the children share their ideas and experiences before entering the Sculpture Garden to look at George Rickey's *Cluster of Four Cubes*. *What do you see when you look closely at this sculpture?* The movement of the cubes may be noticeable at first glance or it might take a few minutes to see any movement, depending on the breeze.

As the movement of the cubes becomes obvious, ask the children to compare the blocks from the introductory lesson with the cubes in the sculpture. Show the children one of the square building blocks to remind them of the initial conversation. *How is the wooden block like the cube in the sculpture? How are they different?* The preschoolers will easily note the vast difference in size as well as the contrasting colors and possibly the materials or luster of the cubes. Hopefully, a few children will also notice the movement of the cubes in the sculpture. When the concept of motion arises, encourage the group to think about how the cubes move. *Why do the cubes in the sculpture move while our building blocks do not?*

Responses will vary, but the aim is to encourage higher-order thinking as children build assumptions about the sculpture. As children suggest different possibilities, explore the origins of their thinking through inquiry and look for connections to prior knowledge. A child's ability to make meaning is rooted in experiences of the past and allows her to compare or make associations that bring insight to the thought process. A few objects such as a small wind-up toy or a pinwheel might be useful in the discussion, particularly as children suggest that the cubes might have a motor or other mechanism that makes them move or that the wind is the driving force. This is the opportunity to explain the artist's intent to create a sculpture with elements moved by subtle air currents, an idea that would align with some of the children's theories. At the same time, it is important to validate other ideas that have merit so that children will be comfortable taking a risk in sharing their own ideas. Explain that they have thought of many excellent ideas, several that the artist might have considered.

A conversation about movement is only part of experiencing the art. Children will remember the art more clearly when they move like the sculpture. Invite four children to become a moving sculpture and move like the cubes while the others are the audience. *Imagine being a cube in the sculpture and think about how you would move. How can you make your body like a cube with straight sides? Do the sculpture cubes move fast or slow? Pretend that you are part of the sculpture, moving with the gentle breeze. Why do you think that there are four children in our pretend sculpture (Cluster of Four Cubes)?* Encourage audience members to describe what they see and then exchange places with someone in the sculpture.

Concluding Activity

George Rickey's *Cluster of Four Cubes* is one of many kinetic sculptures. Introduce the children to other art and artists creating art in motion. *Metropolis II* created by Chris Burden is another great example of kinetic sculpture, and certainly an artwork that brings excitement to visitors young and old at the Los Angeles County Museum of Art (LACMA). The sculpture is "modeled after a fast paced, frenetic modern city ... with an elaborate system of 18 roadways, including one six-lane freeway" (LACMA 2016). Show the children an image of *Metropolis II* to open a conversation about what might move in the city, and then play a short video from the Internet for children to experience the art in motion (www.youtube.com/watch?v=pg-a-yB1coE). Be ready to answer the question about how everything moves (hint: electrically powered conveyor belts and magnets).

Show the children other examples of art in motion using video clips or images, making certain to include the mobiles of Alexander Calder. *Finny Fish* (1948), displayed at the National Gallery of Art in Washington, DC, is an example that captivates children. Look at an image for a few moments and then open a discussion about how this fish might move. *How is this like a real fish and how is it different? What parts of the sculpture move? What causes the movement?*

And of course the idea of movement exists in the art of Los Trompos, although the source of energy creating the movement differs from that moving *Cluster of Four Cubes*. What is interesting for children is the idea that art can move. There are myriad examples to illustrate this point.

> To conclude this lesson, invite children to imagine art that moves, using their own creative thinking. *Imagine that you are an artist and you are creating art that moves. What can you draw that shows art that moves? What will move in your artwork?* Provide white paper and colored pencils or markers for the activity. As children complete their drawings, document their descriptions to add to their artwork, and then encourage children to share their ideas with family and friends.

Conclusion

Art galleries are becoming popular destinations for preschoolers and their families, a trend that clearly contrasts with visiting customs prior to the twenty-first century. This broad, increased interest stems from a growing belief in the capacity of young children to learn from museums and their rich visual experiences. Early engagement with the arts has great benefits. A child's interpretation or engagement with art, while reflective of a child's experience, is just as valid and meaningful as an adult critic's. These early experiences build a child's confidence as a learner, develop critical skills in observing, extend vocabulary, nurture creativity, and pave the way for a life-long relationship with museums. It's a gift that lasts a lifetime.

With growing numbers of young children visiting museums, educators are developing and refining their own skills to meet the needs of this relatively new audience. As museum professionals share ideas and develop model programs, a number of strategies emerge as effective tools for engaging the young visitor, ranging from play-based learning and storytelling to object-based experiences. For knowledgeable educators, it is clear that strong programs use several strategies to engage and motivate learners, and that strategies can be complementary.

Object lessons represent one effective strategy designed around concrete, sensory-based experiences, tapping into the learning style of little ones. They offer rich opportunities to bridge the experience gap that exists between the young child and artists' creations and serve as an entry point to focus the child's looking and responding to art. The range of possibilities is vast for selecting objects to explore an artwork more fully. Toy tops, clothes pins, birthday candles, or building blocks are but a few examples of objects that open conversations about art and connect children to past experience and knowledge that elicit new ideas and meaning in an artist's work.

9

OBJECT LESSONS INSPIRED BY CULTURAL EXHIBITIONS AND INSTITUTIONS

> Culture is the widening of the mind and of the spirit.
>
> *Jawaharlal Nehru (1961), p. 120*

Introduction

A young child's circle of experience is predictably narrow in the early years, beginning first with self and family, then expanding to community. It is in this way that a child comes to understand and connect with his own culture with knowledge gleaned through observation and participation in family ceremonies, holidays, and traditions that reflect cultural beliefs and habits. Culture is implicit and explicit, sometimes hidden in the language and nuances of family and friends, but boldly celebrated at other times. As children absorb the intricacies of their own culture and internalize these experiences to form personal identity, they are paving the way for ultimately venturing beyond their own culture to explore and understand the culture of others. It is by knowing themselves that the door opens to knowing others. What Jawaharlal Nehru (1961) refers to as "widening of the mind and of the spirit" begins.

Exposure to cultural experiences and practices outside of a child's circle of comfort allows a child to compare his own knowledge about the world to less familiar ideas. Seeing a cradleboard at the Smithsonian's National Museum of the American Indian in Washington, DC, and hearing the story of how a mother carries an infant, challenges a young visitor to expand her thinking about possibilities for caring for babies. Noticing a Shetland fiddle at the National Museum of Scotland while listening to traditional or contemporary Scottish tunes opens a new and wonderful world into the cultural preferences and experiences of people embracing their heritage. Likewise, a visit to the Bishop Museum in Hawaii offers an introduction to children's games firmly embedded in Hawaiian tradition, some still prominent in children's lives today, and provides an opportunity for young visitors from different geographic locations or ethnic backgrounds to appreciate and consider traditions and customs that may differ from their own. New encounters that present less familiar cultural experiences are best understood by comparing similarities and differences with personal experience. Modeling a spirit of open-mindedness and curiosity about the ways of others is a gift that museums and practitioners can give young museum-goers when exploring customs and traditions across cultures. In Nehru's words, the gift is a "widening of the mind."

Museum experiences offer opportunities for broadening children's perspectives, but according to research, experiences alone are not sufficient for cultivating genuine understanding of issues of race, language, and culture. Research suggests that explicit conversations are essential for shaping children's values and understanding (Bronson and Merryman 2009) and that non-verbal modeling is not sufficient to convey specific values and beliefs.

Anti-bias experts, Louise Derman Sparks and Julie Olsen Edwards (2012), suggest that through conversations and other intentional experiences it is possible to "confront barriers of prejudice, misinformation, and bias about specific aspects of personal and social identity" and support children in constructing "a positive sense of self and a respectful understanding of others" (pp. 6–7). Educators armed with knowledge of research findings and appropriate strategies for engaging young children in thinking about sensitive topics will be able to support young museum visitors as they explore cultural artifacts and concepts.

Cultural Exhibitions and Institutions

Object lessons are intended to inspire children to think expansively and make connections to their past experience. They are most effective when developed with the idea that the lesson seeks to serve as a catalyst for learning and an opportunity to expand one's sphere of knowledge. It is a chance to broaden a child's worldview to encompass experiences yet unknown, having relevance by making meaningful connections to the child's familiar world.

The framework for each lesson, not only for the lessons in this chapter but for all activities suggested in this text, offers possibilities for engaging children, but always with recognition that a child's curiosity might shift the path of the lesson and create a journey that diverges from that planned by the educator. In this way, the experience develops authentically and stems from an intrinsic desire to know, a process that increases the likelihood of longer-lasting memories.

Object lessons introduce ideas through artifacts that may, at first glance, be unfamiliar to the preschool visitor, yet have resonance with the child's personal experience if introduced in a meaningful context. By selecting objects and artifacts that parallel experiences common in the early years, museum educators will be able to create programs with promise for expanding cultural perspectives of young museum-goers.

Object Lesson 1 Culture

Play is integral to the life of any child and creates a meaningful platform for exploring other cultures. In a summary of research on play, Dr. Rachel White makes a case for learning through play and acknowledges that "Virtually every child, the world over, plays" (White 2012, p. 5). It is this universal experience that frames the first object lesson exploring culture.

> **OBJECT LESSON: PLAY AROUND THE WORLD**
>
> Cultural Exhibition: *African Voices*, National Museum of Natural History, Washington, DC.
>
> *African Voices* is a permanent exhibition that examines the diversity, dynamism, and global influence of Africa's peoples and cultures over time in the realms of family, work, community, and the natural environment. Included are historical and contemporary objects from the Museum's collections, as well as commissioned sculptures, textiles, and pottery.
>
> *Smithsonian Institution, National Museum of Natural History 2016*
>
> African culture is often referred to singularly without regard to the fact that it is a continent made up of 54 distinct countries, each with diverse people, customs, culture, and history. When exploring other cultures, especially those in Africa, there is the possibility to unintentionally introduce or reinforce stereotypes, yet also opportunities to engage and connect children to this beautiful and diverse place. Preschoolers may or may not be familiar with different aspects of cultures from the continent of Africa, depending on their own experiences, culture, and traditions, yet they will likely all be engaged by the topic of play. This lesson introduces children to Malawi, a place that differs significantly from many places in the United States, yet offers a sense of familiarity by engaging children in a discussion of play.
>
> At the Smithsonian's National Museum of Natural History, a simple display within the larger exhibition of *African Voices* shows the creative use of recycled materials to construct toys for children in villages possessing sparse resources. The toys, referred to as *galimotos*, are constructed from natural plant materials or discarded items such as worn flip-flops, old Coca-Cola cans, and wires. With great ingenuity, Malawians transform recycled materials into toy cars, dump trucks, bicycles, and planes for children's play, substituting for store bought products not available in their villages. The museum display shows the recycled materials in their original form and includes the finished toys made for children.
>
> **Background and Core Strategies**
>
> In a young child's world, play is a natural impulse and trumps almost any other experience, taking many different forms that range from object play to pretend

play where fantasy reigns. Play can be a social experience or it can be equally powerful as an independent activity, and is an important part of educational theory and practice. Theorist John Dewey wrote extensively about learning, including child's play, and described children's natural impulses regarding their interactions with the environment and the pursuit of knowledge. His writing suggests that children are naturally interested "in conversation or communication; in inquiry or finding out things; in making things, or construction; and in artistic expression" (Dworkin 1959, p. 61). These interests arise in play and relate to a child's natural curiosity.

While the natural impulses suggested by Dewey are described more fully in broad, play-based literature, this particular object lesson highlights children's interest in one specific impulse, making things. In today's world of education, the term *making* takes on new meaning, defined as "self-driven engagement in creative production that connects with science, technology, engineering, art, and math [STEAM]" (Brahms and Wardrip 2016, p. 6). *Making* is perceived as an opportunity to experiment, imagine, create, and test ideas, and is a natural extension of constructivist learning theory.

The *maker movement*, present in children's museums, science centers, art museums, and early childhood classrooms, acknowledges this natural desire described by Dewey and is becoming an established feature of many educational institutions across America with children's museums taking the lead. *Maker spaces* in places like the Children's Museum of Pittsburgh are child-friendly environments where "the museum's guiding design philosophy is 'play with real stuff,' which promotes the use of authentic materials, tools, and processes in all exhibits and programming" (ibid., p.7). In museums and classrooms, making is a process that is highly valued and recognized for its approach to learning which includes using "open-ended questions, celebrating diverse outcomes, introducing opportunities for productive failure and iteration, and engaging in the making process" (ibid., p. 7). Experienced educators working with maker spaces suggest that "A key part of building a Makerspace is developing trust in the children and their use of the materials" (Bresson and King 2016/2017, p. 25). The same is true of children's play.

The maker approach fits within a child's understanding of play, albeit one type of exploratory play. Not only are children driven to experiment and create in play, but they also understand play to be a natural part of life's experience. As ego-centric beings, children see the world through their own experience and expect others to have a similar point of view. Since play is universal, it serves as a lens through which children can imagine another world. Whatever the description or the setting, play is important in the life of every young child.

In the twenty-first century, conversation about play and its value in learning is recognized by researchers and educators around the world (White 2012) and is a concept gaining greater acceptance for engaging children in museums. By expanding the understanding of play and including play-based ideas in museum experiences, educators broaden their own thinking and increase opportunities to make museum stories and objects relevant to younger visitors.

Introduction to Lesson

As an introduction to the concept of *galimotos*, simple yet thoughtful questions open a dialogue that carries through the lesson, encouraging children to think about play in their own lives and the lives of others. *What is play? What do you need for play?* With a topic as relevant as play, children will share endless stories that include a range of experiences from games and pretend play to block building and word play. In the context of this discussion, it is certain that the idea of toys, from dolls and dishes to blocks and balls, will surface as children define their experiences and the objects that are important in their play. In some cases, everyday objects found in the home are likely to be part of the conversation. Build on this idea by asking children to expound on toys and other objects as part of play.

This conversation offers an entry point for introducing the *African Voices* exhibition that includes homemade toys from African countries of Ghana, Botswana, and Mali. Ask the children to think about the type of toys that are important in their play. *What type of toys do you have? Were these purchased from a store or are they objects from your home? Imagine a time when you only had a few simple toys. Can you think of a way to add more toys to your collection?* The creativity of children will become evident as they take part in this problem-solving activity and will serve as a motivating introduction to the exhibition.

Experiencing the Story of the Exhibition

Invite preschoolers to look at the artifacts in the exhibit and share their observations about what they see. The children will quickly notice the cars, dump trucks, jet planes, and bicycles. *Do these toys look like your toys? How are they the same and how are they different?* Engage children in a thoughtful discussion about the objects on display by asking open-ended questions. *What do you notice about the toys? What ideas do you have about how they might have been made? What clues can you find in the display that might help us know more about the toys and how they were created?*

Introduce the term *galimoto* and explain that it "means 'car' in Chichewa, the national language of Malawi, Africa," and that "it is also the name for a type of push toy made by children" (Williams 1990). The details of place are less important than the broad idea, in this case, that these toys are made by people who live in a place far away in a different country. With young children, sharing ideas in a conversational manner increases the likelihood of retention. Read a few pages of the story, *Galimoto* (ibid.), or paraphrase the book, depending on the age of the group and the time allotted for the activity. Prompt further discussion by asking questions about the children in the book and their feelings. *Why was Kondi's box of things so important to him? Why did Kondi need to use his imagination to create a toy?* Lead a discussion that encourages the children to compare their life experiences with those of Kondi and his friends. *How are you the same as Kondi and his friends? What is different in their experience?*

Concluding Activity

The culminating activity reflects the maker movement growing in America's museums. Invite children to create a toy, first imagining what it will be and how it looks, then thinking about what materials will be needed to construct the object. Provide a wide variety of materials, including discarded or recycled objects – bottle caps, wires, plastic bottles, string, cardboard, buttons, Popsicle sticks – and tools for children's use (scissors, markers, glue, etc.). As the children work, ask about their ideas and encourage creative thinking. *How will you use this new toy in your play?* (Provide appropriate guidance to ensure safety in the use of tools.)

Invite the children to create a class display, similar to the *African Voices* exhibit. Display the handmade creations with recycled materials nearby to tell a story similar to toy making in Ghana, Botswana, Mali, and Malawi. Children can proudly talk about their creations as parents and friends view the display.

Connections inspired by the display of handmade toys in *African Voices*, and through the book *Galimoto*, are rooted in the familiar notion of play, but alternatively fall outside of a typical child's experience in western culture where manufactured toys are ubiquitous. With an introduction to traditions and culture representing life experiences of others in faraway places, the worldview of preschoolers broadens.

Object Lesson 2 Culture

In the early years, children make sense of their world by noting similarities and differences, primarily through visual encounters. Through observation and experience, they discover the complexity of the world; they learn that a single object can have a variety of forms and come to know that simply naming or labeling an object is only the starting point. For example, a basket can be large or small, crafted with different types of materials, and serve a variety of functions, with each different object falling under the category of basket. The generic dictionary definition of *basket* as "a container used to hold or carry things, typically made from interwoven strips of cane or wire" only touches the surface of knowing what the term *basket* represents.

Through media, books, and social interaction, children are introduced to complex, integrated concepts. They discover that their morning orange juice is more than a product from the grocery store and that it originates in orange groves located in warm climates or possibly in a greenhouse. Everyday objects develop new meaning as ties are made to an object's roots. A child's ability to look carefully, make associations, and ultimately compare new information with prior knowledge serves as a powerful learning tool when introducing other cultures.

> **OBJECT LESSON: EVERYDAY GOURDS, PRECIOUS ARTIFACTS**
>
> Cultural Exhibition: Hawaiian Hall, The Bishop Museum, Honolulu, Hawaii.
>
> For more than 125 years we have brought Hawai'i to the world and the world to Hawai'i. Bishop Museum was established in 1889 to preserve and share the natural and cultural history of Hawai'i and the Pacific. Today, Bishop Museum houses and cares for over 24 million historical, cultural, and natural treasures.
>
> Each item in the collection has its own, special story to tell. These 24 million stories trace the history and cultures of the peoples of Hawai'i and the Pacific, and help us to understand our unique island universe.
>
> *Bishop Museum 2017*

Treasured artifacts displayed in the Bishop Museum's Hawaiian Hall offer an amazing opportunity for children to expand their thinking about objects and culture. The hall, filled with a wide array of artifacts representing the history of the people of Hawaii and the Pacific regions, includes feathered capes, musical instruments, jewelry, containers, seafaring boats, a sleeping hut and more, with most objects crafted from natural materials like gourds, plant fibers, shark's teeth, and bird feathers. The artifacts, while specific to this cultural group and unique in many ways have some familiar connections that children will recognize.

Background and Core Strategies

The idea of learning to look is commonplace in museums today, particularly in art museums, but equally useful in history museums and science centers. The ability to use the sense of sight to note change, recognize detail, find similarities as well as differences, and interpret the world is a powerful tool for learning, and one that is naturally developing in young children. This fundamental skill of refined observation becomes paramount in future exploration of basic ideas with the intent to promote more advanced understanding.

Constructivist theorists acknowledge that learning builds on learning where children make connections between a new experience and prior knowledge. John Dewey, in particular, stressed the importance of using knowledge acquired through experience to inform future learning (Dewey 1916) while Jean Piaget focused on the mental process that occurred when past and present encounters were compared, and as a theorist, understood that knowledge was constructed through a process that he termed *assimilation and accommodation*. Embedded in the ideas of both Dewey and Piaget is the understanding that through experience, children absorb information about their world, relying on their senses, with sight contributing significantly to learning, and that experience as teacher, both past and present, is essential to learning.

Introduction to the Lesson

A warm welcome and engaging introduction to the gallery visit set a positive tone for the lesson and draw young visitors into the activity. Children are naturally excited by new experiences, particularly when adults create a sense of comfort and model excitement.

The introduction for this lesson is a mystery box holding an unknown object, a fresh gourd. The strategy of a hidden object is highly appealing to young children and plays on their natural curiosity. Encourage the children to think about what might be in the box and explain that it is a clue to what the group will see in the gallery. *What is in the box? Can we know for certain what is hidden inside? What can we learn without seeing the hidden object or objects?* This may at first be a challenge for the group, but with guidance, the exploration will make sense to the children. *How can we tell if the object is heavy or light? What about its size? Is it one part or many?* Encourage children to make predictions about the object by holding or gently shaking the box to determine if it is heavy or light, one piece or many. Model a sense of curiosity with personal statements that encourage children to wonder or imagine what the object might be.

After the introductory discussion, open the box and remove the fresh gourd for all to see. There are wonderful opportunities for physical exploration to involve the children in sensory learning. Think about sight, sound, taste, touch, and smell, asking the children which of these senses they might use to examine the object. Let young visitors share personal knowledge, experience, and insights about gourds, and broaden their understanding by adding information in natural conversation. For example, Merriam-Webster's definition of a gourd as "an inedible fruit with a hard rind and many seeds that grows on a vine ... often used for decoration or for making objects (as bowls)" (2015) will ground the gallery experience as connections are made between the fresh gourd and dried gourds.

Expand the exploration by introducing a collection of dried gourds of several shapes and sizes that encourage comparison. Include one gourd that is similar in size and shape to the fresh gourd from the box and invite conversation comparing the two gourds, one fresh and one dried. During the comparison, children will likely notice the difference in weight, texture, color, and possibly smell. Remember to share the idea that many people, including those living in Hawaiian or Pacific cultures, found gourds to be important natural materials, drying the fresh gourds for later use as tools, containers, and other purposeful objects in daily life. The connection between the introductory exploration of gourds and artifacts displayed in Hawaiian Hall becomes clear during the gallery walk.

Experiencing Gallery Artifacts

The museum experience focuses on discovery with the children acting as gallery detectives tasked with finding artifacts made from dried gourds. Remind the children that they will need to look carefully for objects that are similar to the dried gourds explored during the introductory activity. As discoveries are made, take time to discuss children's observations and their thoughts about the objects. A walk through Hawaiian Hall will lead to sightings of musical instruments, water bottles, large containers for grain, and necklaces, most objects easily recognizable by the children, but some in a state that is less obvious. As specific artifacts are identified, ask open-ended questions to encourage the children to think more about each object, its owner, and its artist. *What words would you use to describe the artifact? How would the object be used? How do you think that it was made? Do you think there were many objects exactly like this one or would the artist make each one distinct or different?* This is the perfect time to explain the difference between handmade objects and those manufactured. To encourage conversation at the end of the gallery walk, share photographs of objects from the exhibition that represent artifacts made from gourds. The images will reinforce memories from the gallery experience and provide opportunities to compare and contrast specific artifacts.

Concluding Activity

There are many possibilities for enriching the gallery experience, particularly in the area of music. The connection to music-related artifacts from the galleries can be expanded with opportunities to examine instruments made from gourds, from a natural ipu drum to calabash rhythm shakers, and to experience Hawaiian music, dance, and chants accompanied by drumming. The purchase of a single ipu drum would offer a hands-on experience for children to imitate or create drumming patterns used in ipu music. One drum can be passed from child to child to accompany the music from a video. Youngsters without the drum can create the beat or rhythm in other ways by gently tapping their bodies until they have a turn with the drum. Through the use of a web-based video (such as Hawaiian Dance & Music Instruments: Hawaiian Dance: Hana Chant Ipu Part), children become familiar with a Hawaiian dance accompanied by a chant and drum.

Gourd shakers are also popular and relatively inexpensive, yet can enrich young children's understanding of the gourd as an instrument. Children can examine and experiment with making rhythmic patterns with shakers before adding background music to enhance the experience. Although the initial purchase of instruments will be necessary, the actual cost is not excessive, with many options available on-line; instruments would then become part of the education department's teaching collection for future use.

If access to musical instruments is not possible, think about seed art and make the connection to the artifacts by cutting open a fresh gourd to look at the seeds inside. Talk about the change that occurs when the gourd is left to dry in the sun and how the dried seeds are the source of sound in the gourd. A conversation about seeds can be followed with seed art, where children use a variety of seeds from many different fruits to create beautiful patterns by gluing the seeds on cardboard squares. Any dried seeds, from markets or grocery stores to packaged seeds for gardens, will be excellent materials for children to explore and compare, and also serve as an easy connection to the gourds from the lesson.

Object Lesson 3 Culture

We are different, and yet the same. This is the message that dominates research literature regarding teaching diversity and inclusion to young children (Derman-Sparks and Ramsey 2006). With the knowledge that racial and ethnic identity is formed in the early years (Hindley and Edwards 2017), it is incumbent upon educators to promote a message that confirms the universal nature of human existence while also celebrating diversity. Early experiences and conversations about race and ethnicity form the basis for future beliefs and behaviors, and require a sensitivity that values inclusivity as a desired trait, much like honesty and fairness.

Cultural artifacts displayed by museums offer a unique opportunity for conversations that allow young children to explore the notion of sameness and difference while absorbing important concepts about race and ethnic identity. Artifacts can encourage children to think about social behaviors and practices or they can bring attention to concepts such as race identity that might be a topic of conversation that parents find challenging. The end point is the same, to expose children to the idea that people share commonalities as well as differences.

OBJECT LESSON: CELEBRATING DIVERSITY IN THE KITCHEN

Cultural Collection: The National Museum of American History, Washington, DC.

A molinillo is a whisk that was first produced by Spanish colonists in Mexico. They used the molinillo to stir and froth their chocolate drinks. Prior to Van Houten's invention of the hydraulic press, chocolate contained a large amount of fat that was not soluble in water. A chocolate drink had to be continuously stirred in order to stay mixed. A small molinillo would have been used with an individual serving size cup. A large molinillo would have been used in a chocolate pot.

In an ideal world, the object of our desire would be on display or accessible at all times, yet this is not always the case. Creativity may be required to find an object that fits the lesson or experience that relates to a teacher's plans, but is certainly possible with the ingenuity and perseverance of educators. The object described above is a molinillo, a delightful object found in various museums across the country as well as readily available in Mexican markets or on-line for purchase. It is an object of the past and the present. This particular artifact from the Smithsonian's National Museum of American History collection inspires this object lesson, even though it may not be on display.

Background and Core Strategies

Young children are naturally active in their learning and eagerly pursue curiosities. This active approach to learning is seen in behaviors that favor the senses and physical exploration of things in the environment. Active learning at its best is a type of engagement that encompasses body, mind, and spirit in an effort to construct knowledge about the world and how it works (Dewey 1916; Duckworth et al. 1990; Hein and Alexander 1998).

The idea of active engagement requires a child-centered focus where the educator provides interesting opportunities to observe, question, and explore as part of an interactive process of learning. To fully engage the young visitor, it is critical to include personal experience that allows entry points through multiple senses to enrich understanding and solidify long-term memories.

Introduction to the Lesson

Begin with a basket of cooking tools – an egg beater, a wooden spoon, a masher, a lemon or garlic press, a whisk, a spatula, a vegetable peeler – enough for each child in the group to handle one object, and of course duplicate items can be included. Young children will recognize many of the utensils and have some knowledge of their purpose, but may lack names or labels related to specific objects.

Take a few minutes to look at several of the objects in the basket and then ask the children to talk briefly about what they see. *What is in my basket? Where would you find these items? How would they be used?* Explain that the objects are all tools used in the kitchen to make cooking easier. Some tools are new and used today while others are old and used a long time ago. Demonstrate the use of one object such as an egg beater. Invite the children to make the motions associated with using an egg beater and model the motions for children. Then demonstrate how the egg beater works. Let the children know that the objects don't do the work without the help of a person and that it's important to look more closely at the tools to think about how they are used.

Place one tool on the floor in front of each child and give the children a minute or two to explore their object. Have the children lay their objects on the floor and then invite children one at a time to demonstrate how their object works, share an idea about it, and then return it to the basket with a promise of additional time for exploration at the end of the lesson.

Object Lesson Exploration: New and Old, Familiar and Unfamiliar

Introduce the idea that cooking tools are important for all families, but that there are many different types of tools, some familiar and some unfamiliar. Introduce the molinillo, a kitchen tool that is not generally familiar across the United States, but will resonate for some children due to their cultural heritage and experiences. Focus the children's attention on the object, either in the exhibition if on display or by holding the teaching object for all to see. Remember to begin with looking carefully and then initiate an inquiry-based conversation with open-ended questions. *What do you notice when you look at the molinillo? What is most interesting about the object? How do you think this object is used? What questions do you have?* It's likely that most children will have little prior knowledge about this artifact so ideas will vary widely. Encourage children to explain their thinking and provide positive feedback to each, particularly when children ground their ideas in evidence gathered from observation. *What makes you think that?* Metacognitive awareness, the child's ability to understand her thinking and strategies applied in thinking, is a skill that children learn through facilitated experience.

If any child is familiar with the object, invite her to be the resident expert and demonstrator, otherwise demonstrate the use of the molinillo for mixing chocolate and explain that it is common in homes in Mexico and other countries, such as Colombia and the Philippines. Show children chocolate in different forms. It's also interesting to introduce more familiar objects, like a whisk, and discuss the similarities and differences comparing the tools. Children will be eager to try their hand at using the molinillo.

Concluding Activity

Children love to cook and work with adult cooking utensils. Introduce different approaches to making hot, or for children warm, chocolate, allowing children to whisk or mix the drinks. If it's possible to find a miniature whisk or molinillo, children can compare a kitchen tool created for individual use with a utensil designed for a larger amount.

A trail mix of pretzel bits, raisins, and cereal pieces drizzled with dipping chocolate is a simple snack that children can make by measuring, mixing, and spooning the trail mix into small paper muffin cups. By using miniature cups for

> drinks and snacks, the focus can be on taste testing and keep the sugar to a reasonable amount. Children will welcome the opportunity to explore, create, and taste a variety of chocolate drinks and snacks.

Culture and Children: Valuable Lessons

Conversations around sensitive issues that explore culture, language, and equity are often challenging, but at the same time, critically important for supporting children's development. Museums of all types offer opportunities to explore these ideas through their collections even when the connection is not necessarily about culture and society. Science museums teach children about diversity in the natural world. They are a place where children learn that butterflies range in color and pattern, yet have many common characteristics that unite them in one category, just as people have much in common with one another while also having differences. In the art gallery, an appropriate image or artifact can be an excellent opportunity to talk about fairness with children and the emotions felt by people who are singled out or excluded in some way. A portrait of Rosa Parks at the National Gallery of Art in Washington, DC, serves as a springboard for conversations that encourage young children to think critically and show empathy for others.

Conversations around sensitive topics will support children's understanding when educators leading discussions are knowledgeable about cultural issues and recognize potential pitfalls such as stereotypes, tokenism, cultural appropriation, and othering. Museums have the potential to make a difference in the lives of children by supporting parents and educators as they guide children in navigating the complexities of the social world.

Conclusion

Museums offer a wide array of cultural experiences that can enrich and broaden children's understanding of the world. Artifacts such as a wooden headrest from Africa or a ceramic pillow from China offer an interesting contrast to a more familiar pillow made from soft materials. A hollowed-out log serves as a canoe and is noticeably different from a Chinese dragon boat, both examples that stretch a child's thinking about the meaning of the term *boat*. Everyday objects in one culture are seen as extraordinary, novel, or even puzzling by individuals outside of that group.

Culture is embedded in every tradition, ceremony, or event. A comparison of a specific cultural event, such as the celebration of a child's birthday, can showcase similar characteristics across cultures or highlight differences. For many children, this cross-cultural world is likely new. With the support of museums, children can develop a positive, rich understanding of cultural diversity, including the message that we are all the same, and at the same time different.

Museum experiences offer valuable opportunities to explore concepts that broaden children's horizons. The Morikami Museum and Japanese Gardens in Delray Beach, Florida, immerses children in a Japanese tea ceremony, while the American Museum of Natural History in New York celebrates culture through family programs inspired by global cultures, with theatrical performances, hands-on activities, and museum tours. Museums offer a glimpse into the lives of others, and help children see connections to their own lives through interactions with art and artifacts from around the world.

Cultural institutions such as the Smithsonian's National Museum of African American History and Culture serve the community of children and families as a place that inspires conversation around challenging topics. In a recent issue of the *Journal of Museum Education*, early childhood specialists Anna Hindley and Julie Edwards suggest that "Museums have a unique opportunity through objects and collections to offer children a concrete starting place to initiate conversations that illuminate the complexities and concepts of race and identity, social justice, and inclusion" (Hindley and Edwards 2017, p. 13). These conversations are particularly critical for establishing positive attitudes in children as they look to the past and prepare for the future.

As museum educators, there are myriad opportunities to broaden children's horizons and support their understanding of the world and others. For educators dedicated to exploring ideas related to culture, it's important to know and understand the issues and current thinking of experts to support children in this formative period of life.

In the museum, educators will likely discover novel artifacts with great potential for broadening children's worldview and, with some serious thought, discover opportunities to engage children and their families in conversations around critical social issues. Research reminds us that the first step in understanding others is to understand oneself. With this in mind, museum professionals will help shape children's core values around social issues, design programs that see culture as a widening of the mind, and contribute to the overall development of America's children.

10

OBJECT LESSONS FOR YOUNG LEARNERS IN SCHOOL SETTINGS

> Give the pupils something to do, not something to learn; and the doing is of such a nature as to demand thinking; learning naturally results.
>
> *John Dewey (1916), p. 154*

Introduction

Early childhood education is typically associated with formal schooling, even though it is thought of as informal in nature. With the advent of universal preschools and the attachment of many Head Start programs to public schools, it is easy to understand how the early childhood movement is perceived as part of the formal school hierarchy.

In this era of early childhood learning, John Dewey remains a mainstay for the field with educators building on the fundamental belief that learning is active, even as new trends arise. Dewey's submission that "the doing is of such a nature as to demand thinking" is clearly embraced by educators and permeates early learning classrooms across America, even with new ideas of today.

Looking at education for young children over the past century, it is evident that in many cases new trends offer fresh ideas to the existing philosophies of Froebel, Montessori, Dewey, Piaget and others, with an attempt to increase the focus on the changing needs of society. With growing attention directed toward brain research and increased knowledge of cognitive development, interest in early learning is achieving new heights. In the twenty-first century, early learning is more vibrant than ever before with a national commitment to the education of America's youngest learners and with some well-established norms defined for excellence in practice.

A range of models offers choice to today's families with some programs inspired by the preschools of Reggio Emilia and others touting play-based experiences.

Traditional preschool philosophies, as well as Montessori schools, are alternatives that offer yet other distinct experiences for children and families. Practices across models, while steeped in tradition, also reflect growing knowledge about early learning, with insights gleaned from brain research, academic studies, and current experimental programs.

Twenty-first-century Values and Practices in Early Learning Environments

The National Association for the Education of Young Children (NAEYC) is a leader in early learning, providing a framework for best practice. "Grounded both in the research of child development and learning and in the knowledge base regarding educational effectiveness, the framework outlines practice that promotes young children's optimal learning and development" (Copple and Bredekamp 2009, p. 1). As a leader in the field, NAEYC works closely with universities, professional organizations, and associations to create position statements that guide practitioners. It also gathers data from across the field to ensure a broad viewpoint that reflects current perspectives surrounding social and political issues of the day.

In today's world, there is broad consensus among early childhood professionals in recognizing a child-centered, experiential approach to learning as the norm. The idea that children learn best when engaged in hands-on, sensory-based exploration and discovery is widely accepted while educators also acknowledge the value of play, seeing children's natural curiosity as a driving force for learning. Respect for the individual child and family as well as sensitivity to individual needs, values, and beliefs is also paramount in programs of excellence.

Most programs would agree with Dewey's notion that *learning results from doing*. The idea that young children are active learners, or doers, grounds practice in the classroom and is integral to the philosophical constructs that undergird early childhood programming. Although there are a variety of models and philosophies, constructivist learning theory is the most widely accepted framework in education today and is built on the ideas advanced by theorists such as John Dewey, Lev Vygotsky, Jean Piaget, Jerome Bruner, and Howard Gardner, among others.

The Value of Objects in the Early Childhood Classroom

Educators in the early childhood field, and also those in primary grades, give credence to the idea of learning through objects and value the place of objects in the classroom. There are blocks for building, magnifying glasses and specimens from nature for scientific inquiry, dishes and costumes for role play, and balls for outdoor activity. There are containers of manipulatives, or small objects, designed for a variety of purposes. In every corner of the early childhood classroom, objects abound. It would be hard to imagine a classroom for young children without a broad array of objects. And yet, the way in which objects become part of teaching and learning differs greatly across the spectrum of classes. In some cases, educators prepare environments adding objects that serve as props, whereas others in the field embrace a philosophy that focuses on in-depth exploration of objects through a process of careful looking, comparison, and inquiry.

The traditional museum education perspective reflects the latter description of in-depth exploration of objects, rather than the former idea promoting objects as props. The museum view suggests a curiosity about the object and a desire to seek information related to questions that might be implied by the object itself. In classrooms where educators see stories in artifacts and encourage children to engage in deeper exploration of objects, there is a need to model a sense of wonder, pose questions, and seek answers through careful looking and sensory exploration. Children internalize this approach to learning through their own experiences and apply similar strategies to future situations. The beauty of this philosophy is that it reflects natural tendencies that children express in their behaviors. Thoughtful modeling of exploration and conversation encourages young children to think about their learning, which leads to the development of more intentional strategies for constructing meaning in future encounters.

A Museum Perspective: Enriching the Early Childhood Classroom with Object-Based Strategies

Objects of all types – from artifacts and natural specimens to works of art – offer unique opportunities for children to explore and delve deeply into the stories and ideas behind real objects. This strategy for teaching adds a rich dimension to topics that emanate from planned lessons or arise as part of emergent curriculum themes. When educators integrate an object-based approach into their teaching, children explore and learn in new and different ways. Within the field, educators will likely recognize characteristics from an object-based approach as similar to project-based learning.

This chapter offers several examples of object-based experiences for preschool and primary classrooms, some that are integral to a specific topic of study and others that emerge from children's interests or in conversation, leading to further exploration and discussion.

Spoons ... Same and Different

There are many conversations around the concept of same and different in preschool classrooms. This object lesson, exploring the concept of sameness, is surprisingly inspired by the image of *Le Gourmet* by Pablo Picasso and a conversation by preschoolers. Not only do children explore the concept of sameness in this lesson, but they are introduced to the notion of complexity in the world.

In a classroom where art prints are a natural part of the environment, a group of young children noticed a new print in the dramatic play area. Curious about the art print of *Le Gourmet*, a Picasso painting from the National Gallery of Art in Washington, DC, the children commented on specific visual representations of objects – the child, the bowl, and the clothing – and suggested various interpretations related to what was happening in the image. This led to a group discussion facilitated by the teacher where children shared personal interpretations and expressed curiosity about certain elements of the painting through a variety of questions, frequently making connections to their own life experience by suggesting that the young child in the painting was eating breakfast or maybe baking a cake. The discussion included talk of the spoon as a utensil for eating or stirring and eventually led to a question that set the stage for the object lesson: *Are all spoons the same?* Not surprisingly, the 3- and 4-year-olds in this New Orleans preschool class were overwhelmingly convinced that all spoons are the same.

In an attempt to answer the question raised in earlier discussions, a class study was introduced through an inquiry-based conversation focusing on a small collection of spoons. One overarching question drove the exploration. *Are all spoons the same?* A variety of spoons from the teaching collection were hidden in a decorative box and introduced individually during a class meeting, with time for looking, touching, and questioning. Children shared personal observations about the objects. Special stories were recounted about spoons from the collection and highlights of unique characteristics noted by the children enriched the conversation and allowed preschoolers to make connections to personal experience. One slender, mint green, iced tea spoon belonging to the teacher's grandmother captured the children's attention due to the leaf shape at the end of the handle. The children expressed concern about the small size and pointed edges of the spoon, but were excited to examine the family heirloom. A larger, hand-crafted wooden spoon also drew attention because of the carved fish at the end of the handle. The class was interested in the diverse nature of the spoons, including the variety in form and construction as well as the assortment of materials used to create the spoons. One clear favorite was the spoon carved from an animal's horn.

As each spoon was revealed, children eagerly shared their observations and inquiries. The question driving the activity was raised again at the end of the morning's spoon activity. *Are all spoons the same?* The original decree of sameness shifted to a new, more sophisticated understanding that all spoons are not the same. *What do you know now that you didn't know before that makes you think that spoons are not all the same?* The complexity of objects is a concept that emerges in the children's responses. The preschoolers eagerly expressed ideas generated from their earlier experience, noting that spoons can be different sizes, shapes, and colors, even made of many different materials. The idea of function was also raised, with the children noting that the design, shape, and size of the spoon are connected to its purpose. For example, a spoon for straining broth needs to be designed with openings for liquid to pass through. The children's confidence in sharing personal insights was palpable due to their experience and newly acquired knowledge of spoons.

The excitement of the morning's activity led to broadening the scope of the study to build on the children's interests. Time for individual and small group interaction with the collection was included in the class schedule, giving the children an opportunity to closely examine each spoon. The teacher, noticing that one child was arranging the spoons in sequence from shortest to longest encouraged nearby children to talk about the arrangement. This led to individual and group discoveries that included sorting, ordering, and classifying. The children entertained a variety of ideas for grouping the objects, sorting the spoons first by color and then by size. Once the spoons were sorted by size – small, medium, and large – the children made the connection to the story of *The Three Bears* and concluded that the sets of spoons were perfect for Papa Bear, Mama Bear, and Baby Bear since they had large, medium, and small spoons for eating porridge. The storytelling and spoon collection moved naturally to the dramatic play space in the classroom. The playful experience had great appeal for the children. Throughout the day, children were heard talking about spoons, noting that they are not all the same, but rather, are quite different with a wide range of unique attributes.

The study of spoons continued with a class collection where each child brought one spoon to school with each object carefully tagged to ensure its proper return. Many of the children found unusual spoons at home and heard family stories related to the items, and in turn, shared their personal stories with classmates. Extra spoons were provided to ensure the participation of every child. The class collection was carefully displayed following a thoughtful discussion about how to arrange the spoons. When parents or visitors entered the room, the class exhibit was a preferred topic of interest with children interpreting the collection, taking on the role of docent or interpreter.

The study of spoons expanded based on the ideas of the children, continuing until a new topic took center stage in the classroom. Even as new projects became the focus of class exploration, it was clear that the study of spoons remained vibrant within children's long-term memories.

The Bicycle: Parts and Whole

For many young children there is a moment of surprise when they realize that objects in their world can be broken down into parts and pieces. The object known as a clock is really a collection of smaller pieces, each doing a job to serve the purpose of the larger object. A car functions because of the many different parts integrated into the design. Whether it's a clock or a car, children discover at some point in their preschool years that objects can be taken apart, revealing the inner workings hidden from view. Following this revelation, children look at objects with newfound interest and curiosity. This wonderful discovery of *parts and whole* comes, at times, through a child's independent exploration, but can also arise from other unique experiences with objects, sometimes even shaped by a dedicated educator or parent.

The inspiration for this lesson is based on a preschool experience that began with a favorite children's story by H. A. Rey (1952), *Curious George Rides a Bike*. The lesson opens with a provocation, an illustration from the Curious George story that portrays the man in the yellow hat opening a large, wooden crate and George eagerly watching to see what the box holds (ibid., p. 5). The illustration is intended to provoke thinking and encourage children to imagine what might be in the unmarked container. It is important to have this discussion prior to reading the book. *What do you think is in the box? Why do you think that?* The beauty of this exercise is that every child can participate and share creative ideas without the fear of judgment. In this initial conversation, almost any idea can fit the narrative of the image.

The lesson continues when a large, brown box, similar to that in the illustration, is brought into the classroom and introduced as a box that is just like George's. The lesson moves forward with the teacher's suggestion that the children examine the contents of the box together and gather clues to uncover George's surprise. Unknown to the children, the box holds a variety of bicycle parts – metal gears, pedals, wheels, a bicycle chain, a handlebar and plastic grips, an old-fashioned bicycle bell, and more. Under the teacher's direction, the objects are revealed, one by one, each introduced with a question or two. *What could this be? How might it be used?* The sequence of the reveal begins with the least familiar objects, possibly gears, and ultimately ends with the most familiar. The children's discussion and exchange of ideas build throughout the reveal as they explore the box's contents with the teacher's assistance.

Responses and ideas vary widely as the first object is unveiled. An unfamiliar object is a perfect starting point. Gears, particularly those from the real world, fit this description and present an opportunity for children to imagine and make connections to a wide range of other objects in the environment. A few children will likely make the connection to plastic gears from their play, but even so, the object from the box has no real context, and thus requires further exploration by the children.

With each object from the box, the conversation builds and possibilities narrow regarding George's surprise. Familiar objects such as pedals and wheels provide evidence that guides children's thinking. It's almost like assembling a puzzle, piece by piece. Although the idea of a bicycle may arise early in the conversation, the teacher keeps the discussion open. *Let's see what other objects we have. What can we learn from them?*

When the box is empty and the collection of objects is fully displayed, it is time for some final thoughts to encourage greater thinking about prevailing ideas. *If these are parts of a bicycle, what needs to happen for us to be able to ride the bike?* The notion that these are bicycle parts that can be put together is a concept that most children grasp with ease and serves as a platform for exploring the concept of parts and whole. The idea of putting pieces together to form something new makes sense intuitively for children and fits with their experience of block building, art collage, and other familiar activities.

By reading the book, *Curious George Rides a Bike*, there are new opportunities to look closely at George's bicycle, comparing specific parts of his bike with those from the class collection. *How are the wheels of George's bike like the wheels from our collection? Would our bicycle, when assembled, look exactly like George's or would there be differences? What can you tell by comparing our bicycle parts with the picture of George's bike?* The topic can be further explored with a trip to a local bicycle shop to see the assembly of a bicycle.

To further develop the idea of parts and whole, offer a variety of activities that challenge children to take objects apart or put objects together. For example, a simple picture frame can easily be taken apart by moving the tabs on the back of the frame so that a child can examine individual parts that make up the object – the outside frame, the plexiglass insert, a mat, and a picture. Another approach is to provide a specific challenge. *How can you fix this flashlight?* In this case, the child is given a stated objective and the individual parts of the object with time to experiment. Children may wish to work alone on this project or collaborate with friends to successfully assemble the flashlight.

So while this particular study of parts and whole began with bicycle parts and a beloved story of Curious George, it is a topic that has broad application. A walk through the neighborhood can serve as a catalyst for identifying objects with noticeable parts. *What parts to you see in this park bench? How would you describe the parts that make up this street sign?* A visit to an art gallery or sculpture garden can lead to a discussion of parts in sculpture. *How would this sculpture look different if the parts were arranged in a different way?* Whatever the topic of study, it seems likely that there is a connection to the idea of *parts and whole*.

The previous examples illustrate the integration of object-based exploration into formal learning environments. Ideas for exploring objects and collections in the classroom can begin with a simple concept such as spoons or bicycle parts, but can also expand to a study that cultivates a broader understanding of artifacts, collections, and museums. With careful thought and a little creativity, teachers begin to recognize that opportunities are vast and have the potential to enrich any aspect of the curriculum or topic of interest.

A Case Study: Collections, Connections

The first grade team at Palm Beach Day Academy (PBDA) in West Palm Beach embraces object-based exploration as a framework for student learning. In this independent school setting, the teachers achieve curricular goals by leveraging opportunities to incorporate deep exploration of objects and the use of collections into their teaching practice, building children's understanding of museums and their role in society as well as providing opportunities for children to learn specific content. Partnerships with two community museums, Flagler Museum in Palm Beach, Florida, and Morikami Museum and Japanese Gardens in Delray Beach, Florida, deepen the exploration of collections throughout the school year in the classroom as well as in galleries.

Objects take center stage in the learning process beginning with the first lesson of the year. Personal introductions are made using objects that tell stories about individual children and their families, where each child brings a favorite object and a photograph of his or her family to share with classmates. This initial focus on objects seems a bit like show and tell, but is the starting point for the year's study of objects and collections. At the end of the year, each child again selects objects that represent personal interests and identity, but the approach is entirely different with greater sophistication and careful thought about the story and sentimental nature of the chosen objects.

As September moves into October, students begin to notice that classroom collections are present in every subject area. For example, the measurement unit in mathematics begins with a collection of measuring tools – rulers, measuring tapes, a yardstick, a compass, an abacus, a carpenter's ruler, a scale, and more. The objects are more than simple props or tools for measurement and take on broader meaning as the class explores each through a variety of lens. The children learn about the abacus in historical and present-day context, discuss its role as an object that measures quantity, and develop skill in using this computational tool for counting, adding, and subtracting. They compare different tools for measuring to see if an inch is always an inch or if measurement changes with the tool. They discuss various aspects of the tools, how they are used, and who might use them. Exploration of the objects is in-depth and offers students information that enriches the unit of study beyond the process of measurement.

In language arts, it is the story of *My Father's Dragon* (Ruth Stiles Gannett 2014) that is enhanced by authentic objects. The novel, narrated by a young son, tells the tale of his father's childhood quest to rescue a dragon and the creativity he applied to solving the many problems encountered in his journey. The burlap knapsack carried by the boy in his search appears in the classroom, filled with many of the objects that become integral to this engaging adventure. From the empty grain sack and compass to the pink lollipops and colored hair ribbons, the many objects used by the boy in his pursuit of the dragon are more than words in a book as they are pulled from the classroom knapsack. The objects breathe life into the tale, drawing every child into the narrative.

The classroom science center, much like a museum science center, is alive with objects during the study of plants. A collection of seeds illustrates nature's complexity with seeds of various size, shape, and color. Different species of plants offer opportunities for class experiments where children observe, document, and compare the growth of plants as they learn about factors important to the growing process. Nature's specimens introduce beauty and opportunity for making connections to the real world.

Partnering museums visit the first grades at Palm Beach Day Academy with collections from their institutions and also host events in their galleries. During one visit, a curator from Morikami Museum and Japanese Gardens introduces the idea of collections using kokeshi dolls, a popular artifact in Japanese culture, enjoyed by native-born Japanese and visitors alike. In the curator-led discussion, the first graders learned that there is a vast collection of kokeshi dolls at the Morikami, more than three hundred, and that only a small number of dolls would be included in the museum's exhibition. The challenge of selecting specific dolls for the exhibition became the central focus for a class conversation as children asked questions and shared ideas to gain insight into a process that is part of exhibition design. The curator's questions encouraged the children to think about finding broad representation from the collection – dolls representing different periods in history as well as different styles from various regions – and help them discover that the solution is not simply choosing favorite artifacts from the collection. The class also saw the evolution of kokeshi dolls over time. As the group returned to the gallery, the children viewed the exhibition with new eyes and greater understanding.

> **KOKESHI DOLLS**
>
> Kokeshi dolls are typically small, cylindrical, wooden figures that were originally hand-crafted in northern Japan in the seventeenth century, but are now made in different regions across the country. Paint colors and patterns as well as the shape of the wooden figures represent the creativity of specific regions. Although there are differences specific to regional artists, the defining characteristics of kokeshi dolls make them easily identifiable.

By spring, first graders at Palm Beach Day Academy have a clear understanding of what it means to be a museum and are able to apply this knowledge to their work, specifically to a year-end student exhibition displayed at the Flagler Museum. The personal collections at the close of the school year look nothing like the September exercise that mimicked show and tell. With many new experiences and a deeper understanding of museums, students choose objects for their final project with careful thought about the objects' stories and personal meaning, much like in museums, and then create labels to provide more detail.

Palm Beach Day teachers and administrators use the word transformative in describing student attitudes and their conceptual understanding of museums and credit the object-based methodologies woven intricately into classroom experiences for this transformation. According to Donna Tobey, Head of Lower School, the emphasis on objects and collections has many benefits:

> The children make more meaningful connections to what they're learning in the classroom and in the museum, and develop great respect for objects in their world and the role of museums in society. Through this object-based methodology, students take ownership for their learning as they contribute to class collections and lessons with personal objects.
>
> Tobey, interview, 2017

A reflection by first grade teachers also offers personal insight into their experience with collections:

> As a teaching team, our goal is to create lessons that not only engage the students in the learning process, but also ask them to think. During the first year of our Museum Partnership Program, we instantly saw the power of objects

for student learning and the natural attraction demonstrated by students during presentations from various museum professionals. This interest led the team to change the design of classroom lessons.

We began to introduce topics and concepts in our curriculum by using collections of objects, rather than just talking, displaying pictures, or showing videos. This collections-based approach encouraged students to think more critically, using higher-level skills. Students would not simply name objects, but rather compare and contrast, sort and classify, brainstorm and generate ideas, share connections, and draw conclusions without any prompting. As a result, the students became teachers and we, as teachers, assumed the role of guide to help students connect their ideas to new content.

The success of our object-based lessons, or as we like to say in first grade *Collections, Connections*, has not only greatly impacted the way we plan our lessons, but it also has changed our role as teachers. We now view objects as necessities in our curriculum and look for the students to take ownership over the learning that transpires.

First Grade Team: Heather Fanberg, Lindsay Kosarek, Lauran Rearic, and Janice Remington

Conclusion

The object lesson, with its long history, holds a place in both formal and informal learning environments. Museums, as institutions, honor objects and collections as powerful tools for learning and recognize artifacts for their stories that intrigue, excite, and inform visitors. It is the object that serves as a lens for viewing alternate perspectives and introducing worlds beyond personal experience. From a museum point of view, objects are more than the historical data documented by experts, but have meaning in the context of people's lives, remaining important in preserving the stories of our world.

In formal schooling, the role of the object is seemingly less of a priority, more fully embraced in the early childhood field than in classes designed for older students. But there are many opportunities for increasing object-based methodologies at all levels of schooling and encouraging more in-depth learning to enrich student engagement and interest, ultimately increasing learning.

For some, there is a misconception regarding educational theory, believing that theory relevant to museums is distinct from theory applicable to school environments. But educational theory and associated practices focus on the process of human learning and are constructs applicable to both formal and informal settings. Even though assumptions about learning touch both formal and informal environments, there is at times a roadblock, rather than a crossing of boundaries between the formal and informal, thereby resulting in missed opportunities for enriching student learning. Object lessons should not be a thing of the past, but an opportunity to inspire, motivate, and engage children of all ages, regardless of setting.

In looking to the future, the starting point is recognizing social and cultural changes occurring in our world. Technological advancement might easily fit into that category of change and certainly is challenging museum professions and educators from informal and formal settings to rethink how they interact with and engage visitors, including our youngest museum goers. It is time for museums and schools to look more closely at issues related to technology and learning.

11

THE FUTURE OF EARLY LEARNING IN A DIGITAL SOCIETY: FINDING A BALANCE BETWEEN OBJECT-BASED EXPERIENCES AND TECHNOLOGY

> Around here, we don't look backwards for very long ... We keep moving forward, opening up new doors and doing new things because we're curious ... and curiosity keeps leading us down new paths.
>
> *Walt Disney, in Walker (1982), p. 10*

Introduction

Today's children are growing up in a world rich in digital technology, with high-speed access to global information as an expectation. For most children, access to social media with instant connections to friends and family, entertainment, and information is the norm, a scenario in stark contrast with the experience of their grandparents growing up in the 1950s and 1960s. It is a world in flux, rapidly changing with constant innovation in the technology field.

Innovation requires an open mind and a sense of curiosity about the possibilities for change. This attitude is considered by some to be a pre-requisite for success in almost any field. In the entertainment industry, Walt Disney credits a similar attitude or habit of mind for his organization's success: "we keep moving forward, opening up new doors and doing new things because we're curious." That same curiosity is clearly a defining feature of the ingenuity behind technology's expansion and success that is evident in today's world.

The child of the twenty-first century, surrounded by gadgets from Amazon's Echo to robot vacuum cleaners, is exposed to technology in everyday experiences long before being able to speak. With this as the norm, what is the potential impact on how children learn about their world? Will expectations of experiential learning through interaction with the environment remain intact as technology saturates daily life? Will real objects and tactile experiences become a thing of the past as a tool for learning, replaced by virtual experiences on-line? What does this mean for the collecting museum as a place of learning? Conversations on these questions and others are growing in the education world as museums and schools attempt to keep step with a changing society.

Historical Context and Background

Technology is a topic deeply woven into the historical fabric of almost every country, and in many cases, is a catalyst for significant change in society. New ideas and products reflecting innovative thinking can, at times, seem insignificant, but may at other times trigger incredible transformation in social habits and thinking.

For millennials and subsequent generations, the image of technology is embedded in social media and access to information through the Internet. But technology, "the practical application of knowledge," represents a broad range of innovations, each intended, for the most part, to apply scientific knowledge toward practical ends, benefiting society as a whole (Merriam-Webster 2015). From stone tools and the printing press to the steam engine and automobiles, technological advances such as these are recognized for their significant impact on humanity. The latest innovations in technology define the twenty-first century and the way in which people learn, connect, and know their world. To understand the path of technological advancement underlying social media and global communication, it is helpful to look briefly at the movement as it developed.

In the early 1980s, the personal computer entered American homes (Walton 2006) as cutting-edge technology, recognized by many as an innovation that ultimately changed the landscape of everyday life in America and around the globe. The personal computer, launched in 1981 by IBM, served the business community and, for the first time, families in home settings (ibid.), introducing a new tool for communication, entertainment, and access to information to those outside of the business world. As with any novel idea, people expressed concerns, in this case, suggesting that the computer would have harmful effects on society and individuals, particularly children.

In response to some of these concerns, researchers examined the influence of technology on young children by looking primarily at impact on social, cognitive, and language development as well as motivation. A 2007 review of empirical studies by McCarrick and Xiaoming examined the effect of computers on preschoolers, acknowledging concerns and potential issues in the report, but also describing benefits, most noteworthy in the areas of children's motivation and social interaction. One of several reports cited by McCarrick and Xiaoming (2007), *Fool's Gold: A Critical Look at Computers* (Cordes and Miller 2000), was published by the Alliance of Childhood. The report "argued that technology is physically, socially, and intellectually detrimental for children" (ibid., p. 75), leading to serious health risks and a "reduction in human interaction" (ibid., p. 75). Clements and Sarama's (2003) response, *Strip Mining for Gold: Research and Policy in Educational Technology – A Response to Fool's Gold*, discredited criticisms raised in the initial study by citing a multitude of studies to counter the claims, suggesting positive outcomes associated with appropriate computer use. McCarrick and Xiaoming's review of the literature notes the difficulty of drawing broad-based conclusions from current studies and suggests that more research is necessary to better understand the issue and its implications.

A more recent study by Lydia Plowman and Joanna McPake (2012) expanded the scope of research beyond computers to include cell phones, television, game players, and technological toys. In a 2012 article, the authors debunked current myths about the negative impact of technology on children 3 and 4 years of age, noting that "technologies can expand the range of opportunities for children to learn about the world around them, to develop their communicative abilities, and to learn to learn" (ibid., p. 6). Although findings vary, there is data to suggest that technology can contribute positively to children's growth and learning, with the caveat that excessive use or exposure to technology may present a risk for children. From the initial skepticism to more current pushback on the idea of technology for children, there seems to be little negative impact on the growth of the industry.

Change came quickly, and with that change, a new understanding of social interaction. A review of data collected by the U.S. Census Bureau documents the monumental upsurge in the use of technology and its impact on society. In 1984, 8.2 percent of American families owned a computer, with that figure increasing to 51 percent in 2000 (U.S. Department of Commerce, U.S. Census Bureau 2013, Table 7). By 2013, 83.8 percent of households owned computers (File and Ryan 2014, p. 2).

With the increased use of personal computers, the U.S. Census Bureau recognized a need to broaden the scope of its data collection, focusing attention on Internet access, and by 1997, began gathering information using a new tool, the *Current Population Survey* (CPS) (ibid.). By "2013, 74.4 percent of all households reported Internet use" (ibid., p. 2) a significant increase from the 18 percent documented in 1997 (U.S. Department of Commerce, U.S. Census Bureau 2013). Further analysis of Census Bureau reports aids in understanding the factors that influence access and technology in the home, primarily by capturing data on age, race, socio-economic levels, and geographic location of homeowners.

The introduction of the Internet ultimately led to new opportunities that moved beyond broad access to global information to include a new way of thinking about social interaction. The 2004 creation of Facebook is credited with changing the way people think about relationships and how they are formed and maintained, and in 2017 represents "a worldwide network of over 1,679 million subscribers" (Internet Growth Statistics 2017, p. 2). Today Facebook represents personal relationships, but also connects users to organizations, business, and news.

In the past decade, the concept of social media expanded beyond Facebook to include a variety of platforms such as Twitter, Pinterest, LinkedIn, and Instagram. The ability to connect through these platforms can be attributed in part, to the rise of smartphone technology. Pew Research Center documented this increase (Pew Research Center 2017a), showing that in 2016, "seven in ten Americans use social media to connect with one another, engage with news content, share information, and entertain themselves," a significant increase from the 5 percent engaged in social media of some type in 2005 (Pew Research Center 2017b, p. 1). The rise of smartphone technology and broad-based ownership created opportunity for constant social connection.

Research by AVG suggests that this global rise in the use of technology affects children as well as adults, reporting that 50 percent of all children between the ages of 6 and 9, in America and around the world, spend time on social media and interact in virtual worlds (AVGNow 2014). Anecdotally, there is evidence that many children under the age of 6 also have personal experience with technology and social media. One only needs to observe families in public places or in their homes to see the many ways that toddlers and preschoolers interact with technology.

As social media becomes more and more deeply rooted in everyday life, children respond to what they experience. They observe, mimic, and ultimately engage with platforms and devices which are viewed as the norm, forming basic strategies for understanding their world. The growth of this technological phenomenon continues to change the way in which people learn and engage in the world.

With the influx of technology into everyday experience, there are some critical issues voiced by parents and educators. The greatest concern is the broad-based exposure to unknown individuals who may be lurking on the Internet with intentions that are less than honorable and possibly quite harmful to the young, inexperienced child. This exposure rises as opportunities for connections through social media increase and technology becomes more and more a part of everyday life. It is an issue that deserves the attention of parents and educators.

Americans today, and their counterparts from around the world, are immersed in technology in a way that was unimaginable a mere 40 years ago. The introduction of the personal computer, the development of the Internet, and the expansion of social media platforms are innovations that have "changed forever the way we do business and the way we communicate" (Internet Growth Statistics 2017, p. 1). Statistics clearly convey a story of change and document technology's rapid rise in popularity.

In 2017, children enter a world that is filled with technology that is as commonplace as a latte or scone in a Starbucks. With this as the norm, it makes sense to think about the future and the new norm for learning, particularly as it relates to young children. As educators re-evaluate the way they design programs and spaces, it is important to consider the best approach for engaging young visitors in a new world filled with technology. It is also helpful to consider a range of questions. *How will educators blend the new with the old, respecting that the world has changed? Will object-based strategies remain important for educators' work with children or will there be an entirely new script defining the museum experience? Are there ways to leverage innovative technologies to enhance real world experiences?* Whatever the path, Disney's advice seems worth remembering. The goal is to move forward, "opening up new doors and doing new things" that reflect today's reality.

Assessing the New Reality

Each generation experiences the world in a different way, a fact that becomes incredibly clear to anyone who attempts to make sense of the past. Changes in society are evident in all aspects of life and range from innovative products to human behaviors, all contributing to the shifting landscape of human experience.

Understanding this concept of change is best described in the theory of Greek philosopher, Heraclitus, and his beliefs that the only constant is change, that nothing remains the same. John F. Kennedy also described change as an accepted aspect of the natural world, not dissimilar to the theory advanced by Heraclitus. But Kennedy added a cautionary note. According to the JFK Presidential Library, President Kennedy delivered these remarks during an address in the assembly hall at Paulskirche in Frankfurt on June 25, 1963. "Change is the law of life. And those who look only to the past or present are certain to miss the future." With this in mind, it makes sense for museum educators to rethink their practice to appropriately reflect current social and cultural changes as well as look to the future.

As suggested earlier, one of the most obvious areas of change in today's world relates to technological advancement, the result being repercussions across the social spectrum including implications for children's learning. In response to issues and concerns for this specific age group, professional organizations such as the National Association for the Education of Young Children (NAEYC) examine and update policies and position statements to ensure that practices reflect the most current social and cultural contexts, in other words, the organizations are responding to change.

A 2012 joint position statement by NAEYC and the Fred Rogers Center acknowledges the rapidly changing world of technology and interactive media and provides guidance that comes "from research-based knowledge of how young children grow and learn" and looks at "both the opportunities and the challenges of the use of technology and interactive media" (NAEYC Position Statement 2011). The statement suggests that "there has never been a more important time to apply principles of development and learning when considering the use of cutting-edge technologies and new media" (ibid.). The broad message of the position statement is simple: "When used intentionally and appropriately, technology and interactive media are effective tools to support learning and development" (ibid.).

Museum professionals can also rely on independent experts to understand this new generation of learners. John Palfrey and Urs Gasser, leaders in technology and the Internet, provide insight into this era of learning in their 2008 publication, *Born Digital: Understanding the First Generation of Digital Natives* and suggest ways the world is being transformed due to technological advances. The authors acknowledge that educators in all types of learning environments must adapt to the rapidly changing mode of learning where students engage in the digital world with more ease than with the analog world. With new modes of accessing information, this new age of learners will collect information, make decisions, and share knowledge more quickly and more broadly than previous generations. Accepting that digital natives seek and absorb information in ways that differ from past generations is critical.

To accommodate this approach to learning, Palfrey and Gasser recommend the use of technology when it supports educational goals, but caution that "the things that schools and teachers do best should not be scrapped in the rush to use technologies in the classroom" (ibid., p. 246), which is also excellent advice for museum educators. Palfrey and Gasser explore the role of technologies in learning from philosophical to practical perspectives and suggest a balanced approach that integrates these tools when complementing student learning and supporting pedagogical goals. At the same time, they encourage respect for more traditional methods, recognizing the value of "old-fashioned dialogue, with people exchanging views and looking in depth at a topic, questioning and exploring issues in a face-to-face, real-life setting," and see this time-honored approach as essential to critical thinking and learning (ibid., p. 246). The authors of *Born Digital* remind us that there is a place for digital tools in the educational world, but that "learning will always have certain enduring qualities that have little or nothing to do with technology" (ibid., p. 246). It seems that experts are suggesting a blend of old and new as the best path for education.

Other experts and organizations invested in the study of technology on learning provide additional perspectives for consideration. One such organization, the Joan Ganz Cooney Center at Sesame Workshop, seeks "to harness the digital media technologies to advance children's learning" (Shuler 2009). A strong belief in the significance of the early years drives the organization. A recent report, *Pockets of Potential: Using Mobile Technologies to Promote Children's Learning*, states that "The trajectory for academic and life success is established in the preschool and primary years, when children are developing new habits for learning and social development" (ibid., p. 1). The report explores opportunities for a broad range of students and highlights opportunities for mobile learning, including *anywhere, anytime* learning, reaching underserved children, and improving twenty-first-century skills. It also notes key challenges that need to be addressed, one of which is a lack of consensus on "accepted learning theory for mobile technologies" (ibid., p. 5). Action steps in the report seek "to transform mobile learning from a state of uneven and scattered innovation into a force for dynamic educational impact" (ibid., p. 6). Understanding children's involvement with technology is viewed as critical to success and is foremost in leveraging these tools for educational purposes.

Michael H. Levine, the executive director of the Joan Ganz Cooney Center, offers his vision for technology in education and trusts that a broad debate is needed to harness the potential of new ideas. He believes in thoughtful discussion that "considers how devices children now rely upon as their social currency may one day help them learn essential skills for success" (ibid., p. 2). Just as the organization's report suggests, technologies are not a passing phase, but rather a permanent aspect of the twenty-first-century world. For optimal outcomes, research and debate will be essential to maximize the opportunities while overcoming challenges.

Perspectives from the Field

Museum professionals are well aware of emerging technologies, as evidenced by the integration of videos, games, and social media into exhibitions and other gallery spaces, as well as efforts to reach the public through web-based initiatives. Emerging technologies are found in traditional museums as well as children's museums. Decisions regarding technology are not made lightly, but reached with careful thought about implications, both positive and negative, for visitors.

Museum educators are equally thoughtful and concerned about the role of technology in programming, particularly for younger visitors. *When is technology appropriate for engaging children and how should it be used? What is the value of the tangible object in children's learning? What can a museum experience with authentic objects offer that differs from a virtual experience? What is best practice when it comes to technology and children?*

To examine this issue of technology and children's learning, professionals from the museum field, as well as colleagues from schools, were asked to share their thoughts through informal questionnaires and interviews. Participants responding to the questionnaire represent a range of viewpoints from experts in the early childhood field to professionals in children's museums and diverse collecting institutions that include art, history, culture, and science museums. The questionnaire was also posted on AAM's Museum Junction, through its Open Forum, with an invitation to the field. A review of the data offers some insight for thinking about the questions pertinent to museum work.

Overwhelmingly, the data suggests that a balance of technology and authentic experience is optimal for museums. Clearly, there are examples where technology is a stand-alone experience, such as in a web-based presentation, just as there are programs where objects are the primary or sole source of information through hands-on exploration. A strong case is consistently made for the value of technology as a tool for expanding access to museums and their collections, serving virtual guests who might otherwise never experience these objects. For a range of reasons, from economic and geographic constraints to cultural habits, museums are not destinations for every family across the country, which increases the need to find other means to share the treasures and wealth of knowledge housed in museums. Technology is a response to the reality of American life. Even with a strong case for technology-driven programs and sharing of information, America's educators remain firm in their belief that authentic objects offer opportunities that are essential to learning and outside the scope of technology.

Viewpoints from the questionnaire make note of today's practices and show support for a meaningful and appropriate use of technology that is balanced with hands-on exploration of real objects, both in informal and formal learning environments.

Balancing Technology and Object-Based Experience

Anecdotal evidence from the informal survey of educators provides examples of museum practice that merge technology with object-based experience. Dale

Hilton from the Cleveland Art Museum shared a model of programming that offers a blend of object-based experience and technology. He explained that teachers are encouraged to bring tangible objects like spinach leaves to the distance learning lesson on natural dyes, thereby, tapping into students' senses as part of the learning process. The museum adds to the sensory experience by providing classes with objects for student exploration, thereby, creating a blend of hands-on experience with technology. A similar blending of technology with the authentic is seen in the Cleveland Museum of Natural History's video conference programs where specimens are mailed to schools to enhance an interactive video lesson on rocks and minerals. The integrated approach of hands-on experience, coupled with the video conference, garners high praise from teachers and students alike.

Responses from the questionnaire show a shared belief in the value of objects, not surprising given the audience. Even with an emphasis on the real thing, most participants express an open mind when thinking about technology as a learning tool. Comments strongly support authentic objects and scientific specimens as critical to learning, a value inherent in most museums, particularly with educators and scientists from natural history museums and science centers as some of the most ardent supporters. It is the opportunity to learn through the senses that is credited with making an object-based museum experience unique.

At the Academy of Natural Sciences of Drexel University, early childhood specialist Tiffany Allen echoes this sentiment and suggests that the real object "allows children to have a full sensory experience" (Allen, questionnaire, 2017) that has immense value for learning. She describes a program at the Academy where preschoolers benefit from a personal encounter with a preserved shark from the collection. Allen notes that the 3- and 4-year-olds eagerly examine rows of teeth in a shark's jaw and touch the shark's skin when given the opportunity, all within a safe and controlled environment. But Allen is also quick to mention, similar to many other respondents, that technology has the potential to extend and enrich the experience beyond the story told by an object in a program or an exhibit. By adding a video of sharks in natural waters, the context deepens to show the movement and interactions of the fish with surrounding ocean life, an experience that would be qualitatively different from a more traditional display of objects.

Betsy Bowers, Director of the Center for Innovation in Early Learning (CIEL) at the Smithsonian Early Enrichment Center (SEEC), offers another example of technology broadening a child's viewpoint. Bowers describes the John Bull train in the National Museum of American History as still and silent, but suggests that technology can provide insight into "how this huge machine works" as well as allow children to "see how the wheels and axles turn, how the gauges measure pressure, and how the locomotive operates with steam" (Bowers, questionnaire, 2017). Authentic objects plus technology, where appropriate, are believed to enhance learning.

More and more, museums are engaging visitors of all ages through multiple senses, not only through tangible objects but also through technology-rich experiences. At Mount Vernon, historical artifacts are critical to the story of

George Washington and life in revolutionary times, providing direct evidence of stories related to people, places, and events. Yet, technology can offer an enhanced or new perspective, and in this case, heighten the visitor's experience through a multisensory film experience that includes life-like sounds of gunfire, movement, and the cool feeling of snow falling throughout the auditorium. It is the blend of the real thing with the immersive experience that encourages the visitor to step back in time, creating a lasting or more complex memory. The entry points for understanding an artifact multiply when technology is added to the mix.

A broad theme emerging from questionnaire data is that technology, when appropriately selected, complements the curatorial and educational narrative of an exhibition. Supporting that idea is the notion expressed by many that even with the vast wealth of diverse specimens and artifacts in a museum's collections, there may be limitations to a purely object-centric approach and that technology is an interesting possibility for expanding visitor engagement. Within the context of advocating for a blend of technology and authentic objects, there remains a strong belief that objects are critical for constructing meaning.

Dr. Elee Wood, co-author of *The Objects of Experience: Transforming Visitor-Object Encounters in Museums* (Wood and Latham 2014), recognizes the potential benefits of technology in learning and increased access that it provides. She suggests that it opens new paths to learning in museum galleries, engaging the visitor through a variety of senses, for example, by including a video of a ceremonial dance with a display of artifacts representing the ritual. Wood also notes a certain curiosity surrounding technology that draws children to the experience.

Yet, Wood believes there is "an over-privileging of the visual image in our society" (Wood, interview, 2017). In her writing as well as in conversation, Wood champions the object as an entry point for making meaning in the world, primarily for its connection to human existence. In real-life encounters with objects, the senses stream information to the brain, recording unique qualities of the object, such as texture or weight. Wood suggests that digital images might provide a visually accurate representation of an object, but believes that sensory elements may get lost. It is the first-hand experience with an object that allows the learner to verify perceptions gleaned from the digital image. Personal touch or interaction sheds light on an object's scent, radiating warmth or coolness, texture, or weight, all elements that can be described in a narrative, but increase in meaning through touch. A critical aspect of learning, according to Wood, is the verification that comes from the hands-on experience. But as she notes, the topic is complicated and deserves greater study to best understand the place of objects and the intersection with technology in learning.

Dr. Alyson Williams, early learning expert, acknowledges the value of technology, but perceives the sensory experience as even more critical for a child's learning, similar to Wood's viewpoint. She offers the example of learning about cinnamon as an ingredient in a cooking project with preschoolers. She recognizes that technology can provide access to images and information, such as photographs of a cinnamon tree, but posits that "some kind of object that children can touch –

this is a piece of cinnamon bark, this is how it looks, this is how it smells, this is what happens when you grind it, cook it, taste it – adds that sensory level of learning that is so important" (Williams, questionnaire, 2017).

This conversation about technology and children's learning is not exclusive to traditional museums, but is heard in children's museums as well. An interview with Laura Huerta Migus, Executive Director for the Association of Children's Museums (ACM), acknowledges this important conversation and understands the opportunities that technology introduces into children's experiences. She cites myriad examples of technology in children's museums and describes several exhibitions successfully integrating play and technology in a manner that is appropriate and imaginative.

One model with a clear eye toward integrating technology into gallery exhibitions is The Magic House, St. Louis Children's Museum. The *Wonder Works* exhibit weaves art-making with technology to engage children in play representing both the virtual world and the real world. One experience begins with art-making where children draw and color fish or other underwater creatures, but the journey of imagination doesn't end there. Through the use of computer technology, children's art work is scanned and then integrated into an underwater video. Young museum visitors see their fish swim through the coral reefs in the ocean waters through the magic of technology.

With the rise in technology in today's society, there are new standards in the early childhood field encouraging a blend of science, art, and technology in learning environments. It is deemed important for children to be able to distinguish the differences between the virtual world and the real world, and to interact with both as a means of learning.

According to Beth Fitzgerald, President of The Magic House, the philosophy guiding development of exhibits such as *Wonder Works* comes from "the Museum's community-based Technology Committee that seeks to find an age-appropriate balance between hands-on, play-based learning experiences and technology-based learning experiences, using national standards as an overlay" (Fitzgerald, pers. comm., June 16, 2017). The museum describes the technology-rich experiences at The Magic House saying, "Creativity abounds as children work and play together using technology, art, and their imagination" (The Magic House 2017 website). Their goal is to preserve fidelity to learning with a play-based approach.

Petrushka Bazin Larsen, Vice President of Programs and Education at the Brooklyn Children's Museum (BCM), is another voice from the children's museum, but with a slightly different perspective. Larsen is a strong advocate for the authentic artifact and notes that natural specimens and authentic objects represent the history of BCM and its first collection. She describes BCM as "an analog museum" and advances the idea that museum collections "sharpen children's ability to imagine and tell stories as they interact with our objects" (Larsen, questionnaire, 2017).

Diverse viewpoints are helpful to this conversation and encourage museum professionals to give serious thought to what might seem to be competing ideas. In many cases, the ideas can co-exist, even though the balance shifts with varying beliefs. The conversation is not necessarily an either/or debate, but seeks an understanding of the nuances associated with the use of technology to determine appropriateness for children. *Is learning enriched or extended by the addition of technology? Are objects valued for their unique opportunities for learning?*

Many of our respondents, as noted earlier, express an interest in this careful balance of technology and authentic objects. Sunnee O'Rork, Executive Director of i.d.e.a Museum in Arizona, reinforces this point saying, "when technology is used carefully, it augments learning" (O'Rork, questionnaire, 2017). With a history as a hands-on art museum for children and families, i.d.e.a. is now engaging children through a broader scope of programming which includes "science, engineering and design-thinking in the multi-sensory experiences provided with an increased use of technology" (i.d.e.a. Museum 2017). According to O'Rork, the museum uses technology, such as green screens and iPads, "to trigger the imagination and allow children to create" (O'Rork, questionnaire, 2017). With green screens, would-be superheroes see themselves flying through the sky. Technology adds a new dimension to play!

The conversation is not without perspectives on both ends of the continuum, with some museum professionals believing that technology has no place in museums or programming for younger children, while others proclaim that technology represents the present and the future, offering learning experiences that are equal to, or in some cases better than, the personal interaction with objects. No doubt, the debate will evolve as the study of technology and learning continues.

A Look Ahead

Museums see technology as part of daily practice and advertise the broad range of opportunities for visitors to be inspired by art, artifacts, scientific specimens, and experiences that include digital encounters. For example, *The Publication of James Madison's Montpelier, We the People,* makes this point in an article describing different ways that visitors are exposed to history. "Visitors to historic sites have learned about slavery through many interpretive modalities: furnished living and working spaces, both original and reconstructed; first-person interpretation; living history demonstrations; third-person guided tours; digital interactives; and more traditional gallery exhibitions" (Montpelier 2017, p. 6).

As much as technology has become commonplace in the twenty-first century, accepted by almost every aspect of American society, it is reasonable to believe that change will continue in the future. It is assumed that technological advances will continue with the addition of new devices and platforms that will change human behavior in ways similar to the arrival of Facebook and smartphones. What those advances will be and how they will change the world is unknown. But as John Kennedy suggested, "Change is the law of life."

In the second decade of the twenty-first century, museum professionals recognize technology as an accepted element of society and are thoughtfully exploring appropriate opportunities to use technology in a meaningful way with children.

Research on the impact of digital experiences on children's learning is in its infancy, but essential to understanding current and future practice. A focus on expanding knowledge through research is important. With an eye to the future for museum's youngest visitors, it is a bright beginning to a new and wondrous adventure in learning.

REFERENCES

AAM (American Association of Museums. 1992. *Excellence and Equity: Education and the Public Dimension of Museums*. Edited by E. C. Hirzy. Washington, DC: American Association of Museums.

ACM Association of Children's Museums. 2017. "About Children's Museums." Retrieved from www.childrensmuseums.org/childrens-museums/about-childrens-museums (accessed July 11, 2017).

American Museum of Natural History. "Learn and Teach: About the Discovery Room." Retrieved from www.amnh.org/learn-teach/families/discovery-room (accessed September 19, 2015).

AVG.Now. 2014. "Is Your Child Living in a Virtual World? AVG Digital Diaries 2014 Study." Retrieved from http://now.avg.com/children-living-in-virtual- worlds/ (accessed April 2, 2017).

Bishop Museum. 2017. "Exhibits at Bishop Museum." Retrieved from www.bishopmuseum.org/exhibits/ (accessed January 23, 2017).

Black, P.C. 2009. *American Masters of the Mississippi Gulf Coast: George Ohr, Dusti Bongé, Walter Anderson, Richmond Barthé*. Jackson, MS: Mississippi Arts Commission.

Boston Children's Museum. 2017. "Exhibits and Programs: Collection." Retrieved from www.bostonchildrensmuseum.org/exhibits-programs/collections (accessed July 20, 2017).

Brahms, L. and P.S. Wardrip. 2016. "Making with Young Learners: An Introduction" *Teaching Young Children*, 9(5), 6–8.

Bresson, L.M. and M. King. 2016/2017. "Inventions, Gizmos, and Gadgets – Oh, My! How to Help Your Preschoolers Get the Most Out of Your Makerspace." *Teaching Young Children*, 10(2): 24–27.

Bronson, P. and A. Merryman. 2009. *Nurture Shock: New Thinking about Children*. New York: Hachette Book Group.

Brosterman, N. 1997. *Inventing Kindergarten*. New York: Henry N. Abrams, Inc.

Bruner, J. 1960. *The Process of Education: A Landmark in Educational Theory*. Cambridge, MA: Harvard University Press.

Bruner, J. 1966. *Toward a Theory of Instruction*. Cambridge, MA: Harvard University Press.

Bunting, E. 2003. *Anna's Table*. Chanhassen, MN: Northword Press.
Children's Museum of Indianapolis. 2017. "About: Museum Collections." Retrieved from www.childrensmuseum.org/content/museum-collections (accessed July 20, 2017).
Clements, D.H., and J. Sarama. 2003. "Strip Mining for Gold: Research and Policy in Educational Technology – A Response to 'Fool's Gold'." *Educational Technology Review*, 11(1): 7–69.
Connor, L. 2004. *Miss Bridie Chose a Shovel*. Boston, MA: Houghton Mifflin Company.
Copple, C. ed. 2001. *NAEYC at 75: Reflections on the Past ... Challenges for the Future*. Washington, DC: National Association for the Education of Young Children.
Copple, C. and S. Bredekamp, eds. 2009. *Developmentally Appropriate Practice in Early Childhood Programs Serving Children from Birth through Age 8*. Washington, DC: National Association for the Education of Young Children.
Cordes, C. and E. Miller. 2000. *Fool's Gold: A Critical Look at Computers in Childhood*. Alliance for Childhood. Retrieved from http://waste.informatik.hu-berlin.de/diplom/DieGelbeKurbel/pdf/foolsgold.pdf (accessed June 17, 2017).
Crews, D. 1978. *Freight Train*. New York: HarperCollins.
Csikszentmihalyi, M. and K. Hermanson. 1999. "Intrinsic Motivation in Museums: Why Does One Want to Learn?" In *The Educational Role of the Museum* (2), edited by E. Hooper-Greenhill. London: Routledge, pp. 146–160.
Danko-McGhee, K. 2013. "Babes in Arms." *Museum* (Sept.–Oct.). Retrieved from http://onlinedigeditions.com/article/Babes+In+Arms/1481143/0/article.html (accessed September 21, 2014).
DeFelice, C. 1998. *Clever Crow*. New York: Simon & Schuster Children's Publishing Division.
Demi. 1996. *The Empty Pot*. New York: Macmillan Company.
Derman-Sparks, L. and J.O. Edwards. 2012. *Anti-Bias Education for Young Children and Ourselves*. Washington, DC: National Association for the Education of Young Children.
Derman-Sparks, L. and P. G. Ramsey. 2006. *What If All the Kids Are White? Anti-bias Multicultural Education with Young Children and Families*. New York: Teachers College Press.
Dewey, J. 1897. "My Pedagogic Creed." *School Journal* 54(3): 77–80.
Dewey, J. 1900. *The School and Society*. Chicago: University of Chicago Press.
Dewey, J. 1916. *Democracy and Education*. New York: Macmillan Company.
Dewey, J. [1938] 1963. *Experience & Education*. New York: Collier Books.
Di Leo, J.H. 1980. "Graphic Activity of Young Children." In *Art: Basic for Young Children*, edited by L. Lasky and R. Mukerji, Washington, DC: The National Association for the Education of Young Children, pp. 5–16.
Dickson, C. N. 2015. *How to Teach and Introduce Children the Wonders of Photography*. Retrieved from http://digital-photography-school.com/how-to-teach-and-introduce-children-the-wonders-of-photography/ (accessed September 14, 2015).
Duckworth, E. 2006. *The Having of Wonderful Ideas and Other Essays on Teaching and Learning*. New York: Teachers College Press.
Duckworth, E., J. Easley, D. Hawkins, and A. Henriques. 1990. *Science Education: A Minds-On Approach for the Elementary Years*. Hillsdale, NJ: Lawrence Erlbaum Associates.
Durbin, G., S. Morris, and S. Wilkinson. 1990. *Learning from Objects*. London: English Heritage.
Dworkin, M.S. 1959. *Dewey on Education: Selections*. New York: Teachers College Press.
Edwards, C., L. Gandini, and G. Forman, eds. 2012. *The Hundred Languages of Children: The Reggio Emilia Experience in Transformation*. Santa Barbara, CA: Praeger.
Eisner, E. 1985. "Aesthetic Modes of Knowing." In *Learning and Teaching: The Ways of Knowing*, edited by E. Eisner. Chicago: University of Chicago Press. pp. 23–36.

Evans, E.M., M.S. Mull, and D.A. Poling. 2002. "The Authentic Object? A Child's Eye View." In *Perspectives on Object-Centered Learning in Museums*. Edited by S.G. Paris. Hillsdale, NJ: Psychology Press.

Falk, J.H. and L.D. Dierking. 2000. *Learning from Museums: Visitor Experiences and the Making of Meaning*. Walnut Creek, CA: AltaMira Press.

Falk, J.H., and L.D. Dierking. 2013. *The Museum Experience Revisited*. Walnut Creek, CA: Left Coast Press.

FileT. and C. Ryan. 2014. *Computer and Internet Use in the United States: 2013*. Washington, DC: U.S. Department of Commerce, U.S. Census Bureau.

Findlay, J.A. and L. Perricone. 2009. *WPA Museum Extension Project 1935–1943: Government Created Visual Aids for Children from the Collections of the Bienes Museum of the Modern Book*. Fort Lauderdale, FL: Broward County Libraries Division.

Galdone, P. 1986. *Three Little Kittens*. New York: Houghton Mifflin.

Gannett, R.S. 2014. *My Father's Dragon*. New York: Random House.

Gardner, H. 1983. *Frames of Mind: The Theory of Multiple Intelligences*. New York: Basic Books.

Gardner, H 1991. *The Unschooled Mind: How Children Think & How Schools Should Teach*. New York: Basic Books.

Gribble, K. 2013. "Nurturing Curiosity." *Childhood 101*. Retrieved from http://childhood101.com/nurturing-curiosity/ (accessed August 9, 2017).

Griffen, M.B. 2014. *Rhoda's Rock Hunt*. Saint Paul, MN: Minnesota Historical Society Press.

Hein, G.E. 1995. "The Constructivist Museum." *Journal for Education in Museums* 16, 21–23. Retrieved from www.gem.org.uk/pubs/news/hein1995.php (accessed June 19, 2015).

Hein, G.E. 1998. *Learning in the Museum*. New York: Routledge.

Hein, G.E. 2006. "Progressive Education and Museum Education: Anna Billings Gallup and Louise Connolly." *The Journal of Museum Education* 31(3): 161–173.

Hein, G.E. 2011. "Museum Education." In *A Companion to Museum Studies*, edited by S. Macdonald. Retrieved from http://george-hein.com/downloads/MuseumEdBlackwellHein.pdf (accessed April 22, 2016).

Hein, G.E. 2012. *Progressive Museum Practice: John Dewey and Democracy*. Walnut Creek, CA: Left Coast Press, Inc.

Hein, G. E. and M. Alexander. 1998. *Museums: Places of Learning*. Washington, DC: American Association of Museums.

Hein, H. 2011. "The Matter of Museums." *The Journal of Museum Education* 36(2): 179–187.

Hindley, A.F. and J.O. Edwards. 2017. "Early Childhood Racial Identity – The Potential Powerful Role for Museum Programming." *The Journal of Museum Education* 42(3): 13–21.

Hooper-Greenhill, E. 1991. *Museum and Gallery Education*. New York: Leicester University Press.

i.d.e.a. Museum. 2017. "Our History." Retrieved from www.ideamuseum.org/our-history.html (accessed July 20, 2017).

Internet Growth Statistics. 2017. "Internet World Stats: Usage and Population Statistics. " Retrieved from www.internetworldstats.com/emarketing.htm (accessed April 27, 2017).

James, W. 1899. *Talks to Teachers on Psychology: And to Students on Some of Life's Ideals*. New York: Henry Holt & Company.

Jirout, J. and D. Klahr. 2012. "Children's Scientific Curiosity: In Search of an Operational Definition of an Elusive Concept." *Developmental Review*, 32(2): 125–160.

Jocelyn, M. 2000. *Hannah's Collection*. Plattsburg, New York: Tundra Books of Northern New York.

Kagan, S.L., Moore, E., and S. Bredekamp. 1995. *Reconsidering Children's Early Development and Learning: Toward Common Views and Vocabulary*. Washington, DC: National Education Goals Panel.

Keatinge, M.W. 1896. *The Great Didactic of Comenius: Now for the First Time Englished.* London: Adam and Charles Black. Retrieved from https://books.google.com/books?id= sE9MAAAAIAAJ&pg=PA150&lpg=PA150&dq=to+comenius%27+eternal+credit+be+ it+that+he+was+the+first+to+realise&source=bl&ots=kEOrI2S6r9&sig=bLMOv6JlTS13 Xtl7ohLT2-pafEc&hl=en&sa=X&ved=0ahUKEwihi87JpKfWAhVNxCYKHUnfAesQ6 AEIKDAA#v=onepage&q=to%20comenius'%20eternal%20credit%20be%20it%20that% 20he%20was%20the%20first%20to%20realise&f=false (accessed September 15, 2017).

Kluge-Ruhe Aboriginal Art Collection of the University of Virginia. 2015. Retrieved from www.kluge-ruhe.org/about/about-the-museum (accessed August 3, 2015).

Krages, B. 2005. *Photography: The Art of Composition.* New York: Allworth Press.

Krakowski, P. 2012. "Museum Superheroes." *The Journal of Museum Education* 37(1): 49–58.

LACMA (Los Angeles County Museum of Art). 2016. "Metropolis II." Retrieved from www.lacma.org/art/exhibition/metropolis-ii (accessed October 4, 2016).

Lind, K. K. 1998. "Science in Early Childhood: Developing and Acquiring Fundamental Concepts and Skills." Prepared for the Forum on Early Childhood Science, Mathematics, and Technology Education. Washington, DC: National Science Foundation. Retrieved from http://files.eric.ed.gov/fulltext/ED418777.pdf (accessed August 9, 2017).

Loewenstein, G. 1994. "The Psychology of Curiosity: A Review and Reinterpretation." *Psychological Bulletin* 116(1): 75–98.

Madden, J.C. and H. Paisley-Jones. 1987. "First-Hand Experience." *The Journal of Museum Education* 12(2): 2.

Manchester Museum. "Object Lessons." Retrieved from www.museum.manchester.ac.uk/ whatson/exhibitions/upcomingexhibitions/objectlessons/ (accessed July 17, 2017).

Martens, M. 1999. "Productive Questions: Tools for Supporting Constructivist Learning." *Science and Children* May, 24–27, 53.

Mayer, M. M. 2007. "Scintillating Conversations in Art Museums." In *From Periphery to Center: Art Museum Education in the 21st Century*, edited by P. Villeneuve, pp. 188–193. Reston, VA: National Art Education Association.

McCarrick, K. and L. Xiaoming. 2007. "Buried Treasure: The Impact of Computer Use on Young Children's Social Cognitive, Language Development, and Motivation." *AACE Journal* 15(1): 73–95.

Miami Children's Museum. 2017. "Exhibits: Cruise Ship." Retrieved from www.miam ichildrensmuseum.org/exhibits/cruise-ship/ (accessed July 11, 2017).

Miller, A.A. 2003. *Treasures of the Heart.* Chelsea, MI: Sleeping Bear Press.

Monticello. 2016. "Crossroads Exhibition." Retrieved from www.monticello.org/site/visit/ crossroads (accessed June 28, 2016).

Montpelier. 2017. "James Madison's Montpelier." Retrieved from www.montpelier.org/ (accessed June 25, 2016).

NAEYC (National Association for the Education of Young Children). 2011. "All Criteria Document." Retrieved from www.naeyc.org/files/academy/file/AllCriteriaDocument. pdf (accessed September 17, 2015).

National Education Association. 2015. "Facts About Children's Literacy." Retrieved from www.nea.org/grants/facts-about-childrens-literacy.html (accessed August 23, 2015).

National Endowment for the Arts. 2013. "How a Nation Engages with Art: Highlights from the 2012 Survey of Public Participation in the Arts." Retrieved from http://arts.gov/sites/ default/files/highlights-from-2012-sppa-revised-jan2015.pdf (accessed May 28, 2015).

National Gallery of Art. 2016. "Sculpture Garden: George Rickey." Retrieved from www. nga.gov/feature/sculpturegarden/sculpture/sculpture16.shtm (accessed October 3, 2016).

National Gallery of Art. 2017. "Sketching in the Museum." Retrieved from www.nga.gov/ content/ngaweb/education/sketching-in-the-museum.html (accessed August 22, 2017).

National Research Council. 2000. *How People Learn: Brain, Mind, Experience, and School*. Washington, DC: National Academy Press.

NeCastro, L. 1988. "Grace Lincoln Temple and the Smithsonian's Children's Room of 1901." Retrieved from www.si.edu/ahhp/decorativedesignofthechildrensroom

Old Sturbridge Village. 2016. "Old Sturbridge Village Profile." Retrieved from http://osv.org/sites/default/files/1346-HeartoftheCommonwealthbook12112-OldSturbridgeVillageprofile.pdf (accessed July 6, 2016).

Oppenheimer, F. 1968. "Rationale for a Science Museum." *Curator: The Museum Journal* 1(3): 206–209.

Palfrey, J. and U. Gasser. 2008. *Born Digital: Understanding First Generation of Digital Natives*. New York: Basic Books.

Paris, S.G. 2002. *Perspectives on Object-Centered Learning in Museums*. Mahwah, NJ: Lawrence Erlbaum Associates.

Peniston, W.A., ed. 1999. *The New Museum: Selected Writings of John Cotton Dana*. Washington, DC: American Association of Museums.

Perry, B.D., L. Hogan, and S.J. Marlin. 2000. "Curiosity, Pleasure, and Play: A Neurodevelopmental Perspective." Retrieved from https://childtrauma.org/wp-content/uploads/2014/12/CuriosityPleasurePlay_Perry.pdf (accessed May 24, 2016).

Pew Research Center. 2017a. "Internet, Science & Tech. Mobile Fact Sheet." Retrieved from www.pewinternet.org/fact-sheet/mobile/ (accessed April 28, 2017).

Pew Research Center. 2017b. "Internet, Science & Tech. Social Media Fact Sheet." Retrieved from www.pewinternet.org/fact-sheet/social-media/ (accessed April 28, 2017).

Piaget, J. [1951] 1962. *Play, Dreams, and Imitation in Childhood*. Trans. C. Gattegno and F.M. Hodgson. New York: W.W. Norton & Company.

Piaget, J. [1967] 1993. "John Amos Comenius." *Prospects* (UNESCO, International Bureau of Education), XXIII(1/2).

Piaget, J. 1970. "Piaget's Theory." In *Carmichael's Manual of Child Psychology*, edited by P. Mussen, Vol 1, New York: John Wiley & Sons. pp. 703–772.

Piaget, J. 1973. *The Language and Thought of the Child*. London: Routledge & Kegan Paul.

Plowman, L. and J. McPake. 2012. "Seven Myths About Young Children and Technology." *Childhood Education*, Vol. 89.

Portland Children's Museum. 2015. "Opal School: Our Philosophy." Retrieved from www.portlandcm.org/more/about-us/our-philosophy (accessed August 18, 2015).

Rathmann, P. 2000. *Good Night, Gorilla*. New York: Penguin Group.

Reid, M.S. 1990. *The Button Box*. New York: Dutton Children's Books.

Rey, H.A. 1952. *Curious George Rides a Bike*. New York: Houghton Mifflin Company.

Ruzzier, S. 2006. *The Room of Wonders*. New York: Francis Foster Books.

Schwarzer, M. 2006. *Riches, Rivals, and Radicals: 100 Years of Museums in America*. Washington, DC: American Association of Museums.

Shaffer, S.E. 2015. *Engaging Young Children in Museums*. Walnut Creek, CA: Left Coast Press.

Shore, R. 1997. *Rethinking the Brain: New Insights into Early Development*. New York: Families and Work Institute.

Shuler, S. 2009. *Pockets of Potential: Using Mobile Technologies to Promote Children's Learning*. New York: The Joan Ganz Center at Sesame Workshop.

Simon, N. 2010. *The Participatory Museum*. Santa Cruz, CA: Museum 2.0.

Singer, D. G. and T. A. Revenson. 1978. *A Piaget Primer: How a Child Thinks*. New York: Penguin Books.

Smithsonian Institution. 1902. *Annual Report of the Board of Regents of the Smithsonian Institution for the Year Ending June 30, 1901: Appendix to the Secretary's Report*. Washington, DC: Smithsonian Institution.

Smithsonian Institution, National Museum of American History. 2016. "Food: Transforming the American Table 1950–2000: Julia Child's Kitchen." Retrieved from http://americanhistory.si.edu/food/julia-childs-kitchen (accessed June 29, 2016).

Smithsonian Institution, National Museum of American History. 2017. "Exhibitions: Wegman's Wonderplace." Retrieved from http://americanhistory.si.edu/exhibitions/wonderplace (accessed July 21, 2017).

Smithsonian Institution, National Museum of Natural History. 2015. "Our Mission." Retrieved from http://naturalhistory.si.edu/about/mission.htm (accessed August 3, 2015).

Smithsonian Institution, National Museum of Natural History. 2016. "What Does It Mean To Be Human? Early Stone Age Tools." Retrieved from http://humanorigins.si.edu/evidence/behavior/stone-tools/early-stone-age-tools (accessed March 15, 2016).

Smithsonian Magazine. 2017. "A Historic Kitchen Utensil Captures What It Takes To Make Hot Chocolate from Scratch." Retrieved from www.smithsonianmag.com/arts-culture/kitchen-utensil-chocolate-stirring-from-scratch-cacao-161383020/ (accessed March 15, 2017).

Sommer, E. 2011. "Protecting the Objects and Serving the Public, an Ongoing Dialogue." *The Journal of Museum Education* 36(2): 129–135.

Spock, M. 2013. *Boston Stories*. Boston, MA: Boston Children's Museum.

Springman, I.C. 2012. *More*. New York: Houghton Mifflin Harcourt Publishing Company.

Tate. n.d. "History of the Wunderkammern (Cabinet of Curiosities)." Retrieved from www.tate.org.uk/learn/online-resources/mark-dion-tate-thames-dig/wunderkammen (accessed June 17, 2015).

The Magic House. 2017. www.magichouse.org/exhibits/

Tovey, H. 2013. *Bringing the Froebel Approach to Your Early Years Practice*. New York: Routledge.

Tyack, D. and L. Cuban. 1995. *Tinkering toward Utopia: A Century of Public School Reform*. Cambridge, MA: Harvard University Press.

University of Cambridge. November 26, 2013. "Research: Why Do We Put Things into Museums?" Retrieved from www.cam.ac.uk/research/discussion/we-ask-the-experts-why-do-we-put-things-into-museums (accessed June 3, 2017).

U.S. Department of Commerce, U.S. Census Bureau. 2017. Retrieved from www.census.gov/content/dam/Census/library/publications/2013/demo/p20-569.pdf (accessed April 26, 2017).

UVA Magazine. 2014. "Object Lesson." Summer. Retrieved from http://uvamagazine.org/articles/object_lesson (accessed July 17, 2017).

Villeneuve, P., ed. 2007. *From Periphery to Center: Art Museum Education in the 21st Century*. Reston, VA: National Art Education Association.

Vygotsky, L. [1962] 1986. *Thought and Language*. Boston: Massachusetts Institute of Technology.

Vygotsky, L. 1966. "Play and Its Role in the Mental Development of a Child." *Soviet Psychology* 12, 6–18.

Vygotsky, L. 1978. *Mind in Society*. Cambridge, MA: Harvard University Press.

Walker, D. 1982. *Animated Architecture*. New York: Architectural Design Profile.

Walton, M. 2006. "IBM PC Turns 25." Retrieved from www.cnn.com/2006/TECH/biztech/08/11/ibmpcanniversary/ (accessed April 20, 2017).

Warde, W.F. 1960. "John Dewey's Theories of Education." *International Socialist Review*, 21 (1). Retrieved from: www.marxists.org/archive/novack/works/1960/x03.htm (accessed April 5, 2016).

Weston, P. 2000. *Friedrich Froebel: His Life, Times, and Significance* (2). London: Roehampton Institute.

White, R.E. 2012. *The Power of Play: A Research Summary on Play and Learning*. Retrieved from: www.mcm.org/museum-professionals/explore-our-research/ (accessed January 13, 2017).

Williams, K.L. 1990. *Galimoto*. New York: Mulberry Books.

Wilson, R. 2002. "Promoting the Development of Scientific Thinking." *Early Childhood News*. Retrieved from http://predskolci.rs/HTML/Literatura/Promoting%20the%20Development%20of%20Scientific%20Thinking.pdf (accessed August 3, 2017).

Winter, J. 2014. *Mr. Cornell's Dream Boxes*. New York: Beach Lane Books.

Wood, E. and K.F. Latham. 2014. *The Objects of Experience: Transforming Visitor-Object Encounters in Museums*. Walnut Creek, CA: Left Coast Press, Inc.

Zaluski, W. 2017. "The Getty Iris. Five Tips for Sketching at the Museum." Retrieved from http://blogs.getty.edu/iris/five-tips-for-sketching-at-the-museum/ (accessed August 23, 2017).

Zero to Three. "Our History." Retrieved from www.zerotothree.org/about/our-history (accessed August 9, 2017).

INDEX

Academy of Natural Sciences of Drexel University 145
active learning 5, 8, 35–36, 39, 57–59, 63, 123
American Alliance of Museums / American Association of Museums (AAM) 6, 18, 21, 144
American Museum of Natural History (NY) 60, 126
art gallery 71, 97, 125, 133
assimilation and accommodation (Piaget) 11, 61, 85, 120
Association of Children's Museums (ACM) 6, 16, 25–26, 147
atelier 41
authenticity 27, 30, 39, 42, 47

babies (infants) 2, 6, 25, 37, 98, 113
Bata Shoe Museum 51, 54
Bishop Museum 113, 119
Boston Children's Museum 4, 5, 16, 28, 59
brain research 127–128
Brooklyn Children's Museum (BCM) 4, 15–16, 28, 43, 147
Brooklyn Institute of Arts and Sciences 4
Bruner, Jerome 9, 11–13, 34, 58–59, 86, 109, 128

child-centered 9, 11, 28, 34, 57–58, 123, 128
child development 25, 128
children's books/children's literature 75, 77, 80, 82, 89, 103

Children's Museum of Denver 26
Children's Museum of Indianapolis 28–29
Children's Museum of Pittsburg 116
children's museums 4–6, 15–16, 19, 21, 25–30, 42–43, 59, 116, 144, 147
Children's Room 4
Cleveland Museum of Natural History 60, 145
collecting 15, 18, 30, 67, 73–82
collecting institutions 4, 15–16, 21, 25–26, 28, 139, 144
collections 2–6, 9, 12, 15–16, 18, 21, 25, 28–29, 43–44, 48, 53, 59, 73–82, 85, 115, 125–126, 133–136, 144, 146–147
cognitive development 38–39, 42, 61, 99, 127
Comenius, John Amos 31, 33–34, 38, 40, 42, 44
computer(s) 139–141, 147
constructivism/constructivist theory 8–10, 12, 18, 33, 39, 42, 57–58, 86, 109, 116, 119, 128
critical thinking 66, 143
Csikszentmihalyi, Mihaly 13
creative movement/children's movement 54–55, 101, 103, 104, 109, 110
creativity 36, 41, 70, 79, 95, 97–98, 112, 117, 123, 134, 147
culture 6, 8, 11, 15, 17, 19, 25–27, 29, 40, 46, 53–54, 79, 97, 102, 113–115, 118–120, 122, 125–126, 134, 144
curiosity 3–4, 8, 12–13, 17, 22, 24–25, 27, 30, 38, 40–41, 43, 46, 53, 55, 59–65, 67, 72–76, 85, 91–93, 96, 104, 114, 116, 120, 128–131, 138, 146

Dana, John Cotton 43–45, 50
developmentally appropriate 42
Dewey, John 9–10, 13, 33, 38–40, 42, 58, 75, 86, 109, 116, 119–120, 123, 127–128
digital/technology 2, 27, 138, 142–143, 146, 148–149
discovery (process) 5, 12, 37, 41, 51, 53, 57–61, 63, 66, 72, 121, 128; discovery centers 27, 60; discovery learning 7, 58–60, 72; discovery rooms/carts 5, 24, 59–60, 66
drawing 35, 38, 46, 64, 66, 69–72, 77–78, 93, 108, 112
Duckworth, Eleanor 58–59, 123

early childhood education 5, 127
Early Learning Model (ELM) 8–9
educational theory 6–8, 14, 25, 33, 57, 116, 136
Eisner, Elliott 13
epistemology 7, 22–23
Excellence and Equity: Education and the Public Dimension 6, 18–19, 21, 30
experiential learning 5, 38–39, 138
Exploratorium 5, 16, 159

family audience/learning 2, 5, 14, 23–24, 29, 58, 76, 97, 102, 112–113, 126, 128, 138, 144
field trips/school journeys 5, 59
formal learning and informal learning/environments 6, 31, 42–44, 72, 77, 79–80, 127, 133, 136–137, 144
Froebel, Friedrich 31, 34–38, 40, 42, 44, 127

Gallup, Anna Billings 16, 43
Gardner, Howard 9, 12–13, 42–43, 128
Getty Museum 71
gifts and occupations 36–38
Goodyear, William H. 4

Hawaii Children's Discovery Center 27
Hein, George E. 7, 8, 18, 57–58
higher order thinking/critical thinking 63, 66, 101, 106, 110, 143
Hirshhorn Museum and Sculpture Garden 55, 106

i.d.e.a.museum 148
idealism 7
imagination 1, 16–17, 26, 28, 36–37, 39, 53–55, 61, 70–71, 87, 94–97, 100, 105–106, 108, 118, 147–48

infants *see* babies
informal learning *see* formal learning and informal learning
inquiry 51, 62–64, 87, 92, 110, 116, 124, 128–130
interests (children's) 3–4, 9, 13, 16–17, 19, 22, 24, 28, 31, 39–41, 44–45, 50, 53, 55, 58–59, 62, 64–67, 69–71, 73–80, 82, 91, 93, 100, 103–104, 106, 109, 111, 116, 123–124, 129–131, 133–134, 136
Internet 111, 139–142

Johnson, Lyndon B. 5
Journal of Museum Education 19, 126

kindergarten 31, 35–36, 44, 77, 104
Kluge-Ruhe Aboriginal Art Collection 6

Langley, Samuel P. 4
language 10, 33–34, 36, 43, 51, 79–80, 91, 99, 113–114, 125, 134; development 63, 76, 139; hundred languages of children (Reggio Emilia) 41
learning theory 7, 9, 18, 32, 39, 86, 116, 128, 143
literacy 32, 80; visual literacy 65
Los Angeles County Museum of Art 111

Magic House 147
maker/maker spaces – 27, 116, 118
Malaguzzi, Loris 40, 97
Manchester Museum 32
Maslow, Abraham 13
Mengel, Levi 83–84
Miami Children's Museum 26
Migus, Laura Huerta 26–27, 147
Montessori, Maria 9, 11, 127–128
Monticello 84, 89
Montpelier 47, 85, 87–88, 148
Morikami Museum and Japanese Gardens 126, 133–134
motivation 10, 13, 73, 99, 109, 139
Mount Vernon – 22, 84, 145
movement *see* creative movement
multiple intelligences 12, 42
museum schools 78–79, 84

National Association for the Education of Young Children (NAEYC) 61, 63, 80, 128, 142
National Gallery of Art (NGA) 55, 70, 106, 109, 111, 125, 129
National Museum of African American History and Culture (NMAAHC) 126

National Museum of American History (NMAH) 22, 24–25, 52, 90, 122–123, 145
National Museum of the American Indian (NMAI) 54, 113
National Museum of Natural History (NMNH) 6, 17, 59, 115
nature (learning/education) 3–4, 6, 17, 28, 32, 35–36, 38–41, 66–69, 76–79, 81–82, 107–108, 128, 134
neuroscience 5
Newark Museum 43–44
Nicolaysen Art Museum and Discovery Center 60

object-based/learning/epistemology 22–23, 25, 33–34, 44–45, 47–48, 50, 56, 112, 129, 133, 135–136, 138, 141, 144–145
observation 5, 13–14, 23, 34–35, 39, 41, 46–50, 59, 62, 64, 78, 84, 86–87, 90, 99, 101, 104, 108, 113, 117–119, 121, 124, 130
Ohr, George 17
Oppenheimer, Frank 5, 16, 59

Palace Museum, Beijing, China 52
Palm Beach Day Academy (PBDA) 79, 133–135
participatory learning/movement 18, 24, 59
Pestalozzi, Johann 31, 34–36, 38, 40, 42
Philadelphia Museum of Art 6
photography 64–67, 72
Piaget, Jean 9, 11–12, 34–35, 39–40, 58, 61, 85–86, 109, 119–120, 127–128
play: dramatic/imaginative/role play 6, 10, 12, 16, 21, 25–30, 36–38, 40, 46, 53–55, 61, 63, 74–79, 82, 87, 90–91, 94–95, 98–99, 102, 104–105, 109, 112, 115–118, 127–129, 131–132, 147–148
progressive education 33–35, 38–43
project-based learning 42, 129
Project Zero 46–47
provocation 41, 45, 53–55, 60, 108, 131

Q'rius Jr. Discovery Room 60

realism 7
Reggio Emilia, Italy/Reggio Model 40–41, 53, 78, 97, 127

respect (for children/early childhood education) 12, 14, 34, 40, 58, 77–79, 82, 114, 128

scaffolding 11, 46, 60, 63
schema 8, 11, 61
science: museums/centers/education 3, 5, 19, 25–26, 28, 32, 34–35, 53, 58–60, 63, 70, 77, 79, 116, 119, 125, 134, 144–145, 147–148
senses/sensory learning 2, 4–5, 8, 10–12, 23–24, 26, 28, 30, 33–35, 39–40, 43, 46–48, 51–53, 59–60, 62, 64, 73, 75, 78, 80, 83–84, 92, 96, 104–106, 109, 112, 120, 123, 128–129, 145–148
Smead Discovery Center 60
Smithsonian Early Enrichment Center (SEEC) 6, 78, 145
Smithsonian Institution (SI) 4, 6, 15, 17–18, 21, 25, 52, 54–55, 59, 78, 90, 93, 106, 113, 115, 123, 126
Smithsonian's American Art Museum (SAAM) 106
sorting, ordering, classifying 40, 75, 82, 131
Spock, Michael 5, 16, 28, 59
STEM (Science, Technology, Engineering, Mathematics) 25
storytelling 54–55, 80, 94–95, 103, 105, 112, 131

tactile learning 11, 16, 23, 30, 52–53, 84, 101, 138
technology 14, 25, 48, 65, 116, 137–148
Thinking Routines 46

visitor-centered experience/philosophy 15, 28
Vygotsky, Lev 9–12, 58, 62, 86, 98–99, 104, 109, 128

War on Poverty 5
ways of knowing 10, 12–13, 42, 58
Wegman's Wonderplace 25

Zero to Three 63
zone of proximal development 11

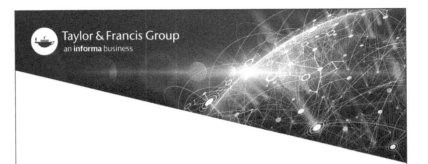